Your Towns and Cities in tl

Glossop
in the Great War

Your Towns and Cities in the Great War

Glossop
in the Great War

Glynis Cooper

Pen & Sword
MILITARY

This book is dedicated to Joseph Cooper (1884-1972) of Glossop who served with the Royal Welsh Fusiliers in the Dardanelles and Palestine during the Great War, to the 300 men from Glossop and 160 men from Hadfield who made the supreme sacrifice, and to all those from Glossop and its townships who fought so valiantly in the 'war to end all wars', 1914-1918.

First published in Great Britain in 2015 by
PEN & SWORD MILITARY
an imprint of
Pen and Sword Books Ltd
47 Church Street
Barnsley
South Yorkshire S70 2AS

Copyright © Glynis Cooper 2015

ISBN 978 1 47382 171 2

The right of Glynis Cooper to be identified as the author
of this work has been asserted by her in accordance with the
Copyright, Designs and Patents Act 1988.

A CIP record for this book is available from the British Library.

Printed and bound in England
by CPI Group (UK) Ltd, Croydon, CR0 4YY

Typeset in Times New Roman

Pen & Sword Books Ltd incorporates the imprints of
Pen & Sword Archaeology, Atlas, Aviation, Battleground, Discovery,
Family History, History, Maritime, Military, Naval, Politics, Railways,
Select, Social History, Transport, True Crime, and Claymore Press,
Frontline Books, Leo Cooper, Praetorian Press, Remember When,
Seaforth Publishing and Wharncliffe.
For a complete list of Pen and Sword titles please contact
Pen and Sword Books Limited
47 Church Street, Barnsley, South Yorkshire, S70 2AS, England
E-mail: enquiries@pen-and-sword.co.uk
Website: **www.pen-and-sword.co.uk**

Contents

Acknowledgements

With grateful acknowledgement to Pen & Sword for initiating and publishing this book, to the helpful and long suffering staff of Glossop Library whose interest and assistance in this project proved invaluable, and to family and friends for accepting without rancour being totally ignored while I completed this book. Thank you everyone.

Chapter One

1914

GLOSSOP WAS, AND still remains to some extent, a typical small northern mill-town snuggled into the north-western corner of Derbyshire about 12 miles due east of Manchester. In 1902 the town was described: 'Glossopdale Rural District Council consists of some places of a more urban character, separated by other portions of a strictly rural and agricultural character[…]a mixture of farm workers and cotton workers.' At the outbreak of the Great War, on 4th August 1914, most of Glossopdale was owned by Lord Howard, the Duke of Norfolk, and had been since the seventeenth century. The area originally consisted of ten small townships. The oldest of these were Glossop to the east (now known as Old Glossop), Hadfield and Padfield to the west, and Whitfield to the south. The other townships were Chunal, Gamesley, Dinting, Simmondley, Charlesworth and Ludworth. Until the coming of the Industrial Revolution, the whole of Glossopdale was a sleepy farming community, a Roman fort its main claim to historical distinction. Stone for building was quarried locally and there was opencast mining for coal. The coal mines at Simmondley were not particularly deep but they were quite extensive and had, at one time, supplied Dinting Printworks (owned by the family of Beatrix Potter, until the early years of the twentieth century) with all their necessary fuel.

The change in the local landscape, which began at the end of the eighteenth century, from farmscape to millscape, was rapid and bewildering. Until about 1780 Glossop had been remote and insular. Then the Industrial Revolution came, followed in 1845 by the building of the railway linking Glossop to Manchester and Sheffield. Old ways, old traditions, old beliefs and the old life became subsumed by the noise and smoke and industry of the 'dark Satanic mills', a myriad of tall black chimneys lancing the pretty valley like pins in a pin cushion. The town 'migrated', mostly to the west, as demand for land on which to build textile mills and workers' cottages increased. The Town Hall was built where High Street East met High Street West, with a market place to the rear. Butchers', grocers' and drapers' shops lined the streets and there were working men's clubs and a large number of pubs. Several mill owners contracted with local farmers for exclusive supplies of food grown, which they then sold on to their workers at discounted rates. Although Glossop fared much better in some ways than a lot of its neighbours, because it was surrounded by hills, moorlands, a number of farms and open countryside, life was still hard, grim and dirty for many of its people.

If there had been unease in the air of national and international politics during the first few months of 1914, the local Glossop paper had not picked up on it. Although the town had become an industrial cotton-millscape, its psyche remained insular, and parochial matters were always of much greater interest than news from the outside world. During much of March and April the main concern was the death and funeral of Mrs Anne Kershaw-Wood, a notable Glossop lady and a benefactress of the town. Letters home to the Glossop newspaper were published from a number of former townspeople who had emigrated to Canada. There were stories of union disputes and possible short-time working in the local weaving trade, sports fixtures and news from the surrounding villages. Although motoring was still in its infancy, Glossop 'possessed one of the most modern and up to date garages in the country[…]the Glossop Motor Company Ltd.' The proprietor was Mr Walter Fielding, a Glossop man who had 'learned his trade across the

Glossop Town Centre (urban aspect of Glossop) on the eve of the Great War, c1914

pond', and who had returned to his native town to dispense the benefits of his experience. Interest in the motoring industry was growing rapidly and business was good. The Glossop Motor Company premises were on Arundel Street and they still house a motor trade business today. Local events and the cost of living and new labour saving devices were the main topics of conversation. The assassination of Archduke Franz Ferdinand scarcely merited a mention. Even in late July the talk was of the local effects of Lloyd George's budget and 'how to wash a tub of clothes in four minutes with no boiling, no rubbing and no scrubbing'.

However, a tense and increasingly violent political drama was being played out on the European stage. On 28 June, the Archduke Franz Ferdinand, heir to the Austro-Hungarian throne, and his wife, Duchess Sophie, were assassinated in Sarajevo (a town in Bosnia which, at that time, was part of Austria-Hungary) by a member of the Serbian nationalist organisation, the Black Hand. A week later the German kaiser, Wilhelm, offered Austria-Hungarian and German support for a war against Serbia. There had been a number of political tensions caused by competition between Austria-Hungary, Serbia and Russia for territory in the Balkan States. Bosnia did not wish to be part of Austria-Hungary and the Serbs wanted to take over Bosnia for themselves. On 23 July, Austria-Hungary gave the Serbs an ultimatum, which they largely ignored, and on 28 July, Austria-Hungary declared war against the Serbs.

To everyone's surprise Russia mobilised troops. On 31 July, Germany warned Russia about mobilising troops but the Russians insisted that their mobilisation was directed at Austria-Hungary alone. Clearly not believing this, the Germans declared war on Russia the following day and then signed a secret alliance treaty with the Ottoman Empire. The next day, 2 August, Germany invaded Luxembourg and the first military skirmish on the Western Front took place at Joncherey. On 3 August, Germany declared war on France and demanded that Belgium allowed German arms to reach the French border. The Belgians, as per their neutral status, refused to do so, and on 4 August, Germany invaded Belgium. Britain protested at this violation of Belgian neutrality, which was guaranteed by a treaty. The German chancellor dismissed British objections saying that the treaty was 'just a scrap of paper'. Incensed, the British declared war on Germany. The following day the Ottomans closed the Dardanelles and the scene was set for the greatest war in history.

Finally, on 3 August, Glossop woke up to the very real threat of war. 'Armageddon[…]the coming crisis' ran the headline in the *Glossop Chronicle*. The following day, what became known as the Great War was officially declared. A week later France declared war on Austria-Hungary and the following day Britain did the same thing. As if to make up for not warning the townspeople in advance, the Chronicle worked itself into an immediate patriotic frenzy. There were requests for all young unmarried men to enlist in the army and a reminder to their parents that 'it is your duty[…]to send[…]your sons to the Front', then the following week the newspaper criticised 'the unpatriotic rush for stores', which was happening, despite government reassurances that trade routes would be kept open, at least to the West. The Chronicle thundered that 'there was no excuse for panic'. However, the paper insisted, there was a need to economise and undertake careful housekeeping to help the war effort and offered the following thrifty tips:

- Simple one course meals would conserve both food and fuel.
- Bacon and eggs should be replaced by porridge for breakfast.
- Potato skins could be eaten as well.
- Dripping should replace butter wherever possible.
- And bread and jam should be eaten without butter.

Most millworker's families already practised these economies out of necessity, but they would have come as a shock to those who were better off. Meantime, the Co-operative Wholesale Society worried about the price of flour and sugar. Farmers and smallholders were also strongly advised that their hens should not be kept for more than a year and that any sizeable pig should be killed, which noticeably affected a number of farms in the Glossop area.

It is said that a week is a long time in politics but to the bewildered and bemused townsfolk of Glossop it must have been one of the longest and most agonising weeks of their lives. Within the space of a few days their entire world had been turned upside-down without much warning. It seemed that food might be under threat of rationing and there were all these new rules and regulations to be heeded. Suddenly nothing was certain any more. The menfolk, who were often the breadwinners of the family, were urged to leave their families and their jobs, to give up the life that they had known, to go and fight an enemy in a foreign land for a cause they really did not fully understand. Many felt they were duty-bound to go on the grounds of both personal and national honour. Wives

Cavalry non-commissioned officers in the Great War, c1915.

and children, parents and siblings would be left to manage as best they could, in reduced circumstances, knowing that their loved ones would be going to war and might never return home. This must have been a terrifying prospect, especially before the days of the welfare state and mass media communications.

In 1876, Captain William Sidebottom formed the 23rd Derbyshire Rifle Volunteer Corps (RVC) in Glossop. In 1880, the 23rd Derbyshire RVC was incorporated into D Company of the 1st Admin Battalion 4th Cheshires, which was then re-named the 4th Cheshire (Cheshire and Derbyshire) Rifle Volunteer Corps. In December 1887, this became the 4th Volunteer Battalion Cheshire Regiment and when the Territorial Force was formed in 1908, the name changed yet again to become the 6th Battalion Cheshire Regiment. General opinion seemed to be that the war would not last very long and existing members of the Glossop contingent of the regiment were the first men from the town to report and volunteer for active service. However, it rapidly became clear that these numbers would be pitifully insufficient and that many more men would be required to enlist. The call went out. Initially there was an enthusiastic response from men eager and willing to defend themselves, their families and their country's honour. Enlisters were sent to Cambridge for full training before being shipped out to the Front. They went cheerfully enough, certain that, once they had taught the Germans a lesson, they would be home in time for Christmas. But the war was less than a month old before Glossop received news of the first casualty from the town. Able Seaman Amos Barton, serving on the destroyer HMS *Kenneth*, was wounded in action against a German destroyer. The German Navy was of at least equal strength to the British Navy and the Germans were prepared for war. The British, who had not thought it would come to war and, even if it did, had not expected to be involved, were 'caught on the hop' and ill-prepared.

It quickly became obvious that the army was also ill-prepared and ill-equipped to fight battles. The war had been barely three weeks into its course before Glossop people were being warned of 'the prospect of a long, arduous and severe struggle'. Queen Mary appealed to the country's needlework guilds for socks, nightshirts, pyjamas and operation gowns as well as clothing for women and children. Glossop had several sewing circles, the largest of which was the mayoress's needlework group, and there was also a thriving one in the name of Mrs Anne Kershaw-Wood, a name that was retained throughout the war even though she had died before it began. The Glossop branch of the Red Cross also began to hold sewing meetings to make garments for soldiers. The government provided wool and cotton thread and fabrics. The local ladies provide their labour and their skill. Working men had their clubs but for many women the sewing circles were a much-needed social outlet as well as an opportunity to help the war effort. Nursing skills were also in demand and Chapel-en-le-Frith Board of Guardians (a few miles away) set up practical nursing classes for women that Glossop women could attend as well.

Those not enlisting tried hard to help on a practical scale. Employers vowed to look after the dependants of those on active service and gave a guarantee of jobs for men returning from the forces. Dinting Printworks, which had been established by Edmund Potter, the grandfather of the internationally acclaimed children's writer Beatrix Potter, paid 10 shillings per week to the dependants of those on active service who had formerly worked for the printworks. Ten shillings was worth about £22 at modern-day values. National Health Insurance contribution cards were to be marked 'called-up', as were any arrears notices sent to men who were away in the army. Army and navy war claims would be paid reasonably promptly by the assurance companies. 'Separation allowances' were also paid by the government through the Post Office to soldiers' families. Proceeds from the local Whitfield well-dressing festival in the late summer of 1914 were sent to a general war fund and the Glossop free churches also set up a war appeal. A number of war relief funds were established and there were relief working parties set up by the Red Cross and women's organisations.

By early September no one was in any doubt as to the seriousness of the situation. The local paper had at least begun to publish a brief but regular war diary. On 23 August, the Battle of Mons had taken place. It was the first battle of the war between the British and the Germans on the Western Front and ended with the British in retreat. The First Battle of the Marne was fought on 5 September and halted the German advance on Paris. The Allies were encouraged but not for long because on 28 September, the Germans besieged Antwerp and finally captured it a few days later on 10 October. In Keighley, across the West Yorkshire border from Glossop, an angry mob attacked and destroyed a shop belonging to a German citizen. A plea was made for further food economies and all farmers were asked to triple the corn crop for 1915. However, Glossop soil is acidic with a low ph factor and consequently not very suitable for grains, so local farmers grew other crops instead. Potatoes and beans grew well and so did root vegetables and celery. Anxious that there should be no food waste it was advised by the government that all windfalls and small or misshapen produce should be used, and that cooks should 'stew stale bread, washed potato peelings, the outer leaves of cabbages and old vegetables with a little water, then strain the mixture through a sieve and it would give a tasty dish to eke out a meal with another vegetable', although it is not recorded whether many followed this advice for such an unappetising mixture. The farmers' wives doubtless fed the pigs and hens with any scraps instead and in poorer families there was not much waste in any case.

Glossop townspeople had begun to debate about whether they should continue to support the football team who, at that point, were in Division Two. Some felt that it was altogether too frivolous to play football matches when local lads were out there defending the realm and getting themselves killed or injured for it. Others took the view that sporting activities were a healthy and welcome distraction that should be encouraged at such a time. A few weeks later, Glossop FC announced that it was 'in crisis' due to men being away at war, bad trade and loss of funds. Their Division Two status was hanging in the balance, threatened by a general lack of support and money and, besides, there was no money to pay the players' wages. Although the Whitfield well-dressing celebrations went ahead as usual, there were further dark murmurings that it was a needless waste of resources despite providing some local enjoyment and encouraging morale. Well-dressings were religiously based festivals giving thanks for an ample supply of clean

Model Farm owned by Lord Howard near Glossop town centre, c1920.

water throughout the year in much the same way that harvest thanksgiving celebrated the successful production of foodstuffs. Whitfield Well was always dressed in the brilliant purple heather growing in profusion on the moors above Glossop and it was one of the last in the annual well-dressing calendar. It was customary to decorate each well-dressing with a picture based on some current theme or happening, which was made by pressing the heather and some flower petals into moist clay. Although well-dressing had its origins in pagan times, the festival had been Christianised since the seventeenth century and the local clergy turned out to hold services blessing the wells and the water that they provided. There was usually a procession before the

service and a carnival feeling attended the whole day.

One of the most immediate effects of the outbreak of war was the cessation of trade with Germany and Austria and the loss of those markets. Payments from German companies ceased abruptly. Isaac Jackson at Hawkshead Mill lost not only his best markets but payments worth several thousand pounds. In 1914, £1,000 would be worth over £43,000, so he lost a great deal of money. Initially the cotton trade benefitted from the demand for uniforms and cotton operatives gave up their Wakes holidays in mid-late August to fulfil the orders and also to exercise economies as they'd been asked to do. Flannel manufacturers benefitted but calico printing, dyeing, bleaching and finishing works closed. Local retailers were urged not to dismiss their staff. It was a time of great uncertainty. Families found themselves either on greatly reduced incomes or without their breadwinners altogether as the menfolk began to enlist in the army. Seaside resort bookings for the annual Wakes holidays plummeted as people tried to conserve what money they had for the lean months that they suspected lay ahead. Blackpool in particular suffered badly from the sudden and unexpected drop in bookings from towns like Glossop.

In mid-September, news began to come through to Glossop of 'terrible scenes on the Marne battlefield' and of 'trenches of dead'. There was a flurry of increased recruiting activity as the realisation dawned on most that this wasn't going to be a case of a few quick skirmishes. This was a deadly war on a large scale. The 'enemy', Germany and Austria, were two strong, wealthy, powerful nations who were well-prepared for war. France and Belgium, where much of the European fighting took place and where large areas of country were laid waste, and Britain, were ill-prepared for battle, mainly because they had not been expecting it, although the international situation had been delicate for some time. After the Battle of Mons, during which one Glossop soldier was wounded and another taken prisoner, there was little doubt that this was going to be an extremely bloody conflict and that Belgium was taking the initial brunt of it. There was a growing number of reports of casualties and 'the terrible effects of shrapnel'. Refugees and wounded soldiers from Belgium began arriving in Glossop. They were given 'sanctuary and shelter' at Shaw House on Shaw Street and at Partington Convalescent Home, and a Belgian relief fund was set up. There were repeated calls to arms for 'preserving Belgian neutrality', and more Glossop families saw their husbands, sons and brothers march off to war.

There is, of course, always another side to human nature, even to tragedies such as a war on this scale, and this was shown in perversity. Some was understandable. The cotton industry was beginning to become badly affected. It was urged that there should be reserve cotton suppliers and the raw cotton reserve issue was being widely debated. Glossop, Hyde and Hadfield Weavers Association were deeply concerned about 'the privations and anxieties caused by war', and there was a hint that industrial action might be forthcoming. It wasn't necessarily a case of personal greed or selfishness. Members were genuinely concerned by the rapidly rising cost of food and fuel and the loss of a breadwinner for many families. Much less understandable was the perversity shown in the raiding of Glossop gardens and orchards using the war as an excuse for theft and vandalism. As yet there were no particular food shortages but many people relied to some extent on what they could grow. Liberal consumption of alcohol had been for some time both a national and a local problem. There was a lot of drinking done in the local pubs and clubs of Glossop and there were many scenes of drunkenness and bad behaviour, not to mention a number of arrests. Glossop West End Working Men's Club was struck off the register for 'excessive drinking, indecency and gambling'. A number of Temperance Societies existed, notably the Salvation Army, who preached against the 'evils of drink', the harm and hardships which it inflicted on the families of those who drank to excess. However, then, as now, many people simply turned a deaf ear.

The Battle of Armentieres began on 13 October and ended on 2 November, with the British capturing the town as part of their strategy to re-take Lille from the Germans. In the later part of October, the First Battle of Ypres prevented the Germans from reaching the coast at Calais and Dunkirk and on 2 November, the British began a naval blockade of Germany. Three days later both France and Britain declared war on the Ottoman Empire. As the year drew to a close the war news got more

Wood's Hospital Howard Park, Glossop, close to Partington Hospital, 1915.

intense. In early November a journalist declared it 'the world's greatest war', and wrote of the unbelievable horrors of trench warfare, squelching through mud, water and decomposing human remains. He also wrote of the 'gallant tars guarding our shores'. Glossop folk organised collections of food, money, clothing and cigarettes to be sent in Christmas boxes to those serving in Belgium. There were several funds, the largest being that of the mayoress, and it was she who organised the sending of each parcel to the soldiers who would be spending the festive season far away from their families, often fighting for their lives. While the local medical officers were worrying themselves about the rising number of cases of tuberculosis and a declining birth rate, the main concern for most Glossop families was that of the welfare of loved ones at the Front. On Christmas Eve the *Glossop Chronicle* tried to be upbeat and wished its readers 'a happy and joyous Christmas', only to report the death of a well-known and popular Glossop historian, Robert Hamnett, as well as the growing number of casualties from the War. It was a sombre time, although most tried to keep their spirits up, believing that the military matters would soon be settled, and that the New Year would bring fresh hope.

Chapter Two

1915

THE CHRISTMAS AND New Year period in Glossop was relatively cheerful and there were plenty of parties at local schools and institutions. Wounded Belgian soldiers and Belgian refuges were arriving in ever greater numbers in the town and they were given a traditional Christmas dinner with turkey and sausages donated by one of the local JPs, and a cake sent from Miss Turner on High Street East. The well known music hall owner of the day, Mr T. Allan Edwardes, re-opened the refurbished Glossop Electric Palace on George Street. The new cinema would continue to show films throughout the war. Glossop people had made 'a splendid response' to the mayoress's Christmas gift fund for local soldiers and sailors and a long list of donations was published in the *Glossop Chronicle*. Also published were fulsome letters of grateful thanks from the troops. Stoker Edward Travis on HMS *Queen Mary* wrote expressing both his thanks and his 'hopes of returning to dear old Glossop with a victorious end of this great crisis'. Private Sydney Adshead wrote of his 'physical pleasure at receiving a parcel of goodies as for twelve weeks I have lived on bread, corned beef and cocoa for breakfast', while C. Goddard aboard HMS *Ajax* said 'words cannot convey the joy and pleasure I felt on opening it [his parcel] [...]we[...]are even more convinced of victory now than ever'.

The first Zeppelin raid on Britain was marked on 19 January when Yarmouth and Kings Lynn on the east coast were bombed. Five days later the naval battle of Dogger Bank took place. The British won but without inflicting as much damage on the German fleet as they had hoped. In early February the Germans began using submarine warfare against Merchant Navy ships.

Keeping up morale was important and, as continuing pleas were made for young male, preferably unmarried, conscripts, the *Glossop Chronicle* continued to publish a series of 'thrilling deeds by the Empire's sons'. The Glossop Territorials were showing plenty of bravery and endurance in the trenches and the Manchester Regiment, based in nearby Ashton, was making strenuous recruiting efforts. Glossop Companies of the 6th (2nd Reserve Battalion) Cheshire Regiment trained in Cambridge and the first group of these left Glossop in early February, 1915. The

War horses in the Great War, c1916.

Cheshire Battalion, in their pleas for call-up, were offering allowances for families, in addition to a separation allowance, which was paid by the government to the dependants of those who enlisted in the armed forces. This was important as men who were breadwinners had to consider what would happen to their wives, children, parents or siblings if they enlisted. Another problem was that employers were not keen on all their fit male workers leaving to serve in the forces and resisted strongly, saying that certain key workers simply could not be spared. A call went out to employers to show their patriotism by

allowing any of their workers to enlist, fit or not so fit.

A rare piece of encouraging news was that separation allowances were to be increased and the numbers of those eligible to receive them broadened. Soldier's wives now received 5/- (£8.75) per child instead of the former 2s 6d (£4.37). For two children they received 8s 6d (£14.88) and 2/- (£3.50) for each additional child. All allowances were now payable for children up to 16 (instead of 14 as previously) and they were payable in respect of any child the absent soldier had been maintaining as a member of the household. Dependants were now defined as any person who had been dependent on a soldier or sailor, irrespective of whether there was a relationship. However, payments often had to be made without a proper address being given. One problem was that the war was responsible for many changes of tenancies because as breadwinners enlisted, families doubled up for the sake of economy.

The loss of manpower was already beginning to cause problems. Hadfield & District Weavers Association, in one of the Glossop townships, lamented the 'heavy loss on working' due to the effects of the war. There was talk of short-time working and every full-time worker was required to pay a tuppence levy (about 88p) per week towards stoppage benefits. Two extra holidays were granted, on Easter Monday and 26 December, in addition to Whitsuntide and the Wakes, to ease the problem. Employers did not pay for holiday leave and so would not need to pay out benefits for extra holidays. Glossop Winders and Weavers Association noted that 'these were disastrous times for the trades unions', and that their funding was very low due to the war badly affecting the cotton trade, serious short-time working and the numbers joining the army. Kinder Printworks and Clough Mills in Little Hayfield, just 3 or 4 miles from Glossop, closed down. Little Hayfield was a small village. There was no alternative employment locally so workers had to move away, some to other parts of the country. Although the war had opened up new opportunities for the linen trade, as the former principal markets for German and Austrian linen had been the USA and this trade had now collapsed, it was not something of which Glossop could particularly take advantage. Flax did not grow well, and the nearest flax-growing area was on the Cheshire Plain. In addition the mills were geared towards manufacturing cotton materials. The hatting trade also benefitted from the war, mainly due to the demand for army and navy headwear, but that was seen as the province of nearby Ashton, Hyde and Stockport, not Glossop.

The Germans were busy making great efforts to adversely affect

Britain and its trade by sinking as many merchant ships as possible and, by February 1915, as well as a cotton famine, there was a threatened coal famine. Suggestions were made that the German example should be followed and that coke should be used for kitchen ranges and manufacturing, and possibly as fuel for steam engines, as it was said to be much more efficient. There was also a transport problem because horses had been commandeered for the army and the supply of horses was almost exhausted, both for use in battle and for haulage purposes. The beautiful and realistic film of Michael Morpurgo's novel War Horse perfectly illustrates the role of horses in the Great War, although it proved to be the last major war in which horses played a part. There was quite a lot of open-cast mining for coal in the Glossop area, but the mills took precedence for the fuel and many workers were left to manage as best they could. Food prices were rising as well, especially those of fresh foodstuffs. A basket of provisions, which before the war had cost 10 shillings (about £17.50), now cost 15 shillings (about £26.75). This caused real hardship, especially as mills were going on short-time working, jobs were being lost, and breadwinners were enlisting in the forces. Shortages were threatened and the government began a 'grow your own campaign'. Glossop, partly rural and surrounded by farms,

Glossop township of Chunal (agricultural aspects of Glossop) during the Great War, c1918.

GNAT HOLE, GLOSSOP.

already had a number of allotments but the town was keen to comply and the *Glossop Chronicle* published a list of vegetables to be grown. These included French beans, runner beans, broad beans, turnips, swedes, carrots, onions, leeks, cabbages, cauliflower, marrows, parsnips and especially potatoes. In addition, town dwellers were asked to turn their gardens into small market gardens and to grow salad vegetables, lettuce and chicory. There were to be no flowers. Glossop school teacher, Vic Furniss, who was serving in France, wrote a letter in support of this venture to the local paper, stating that 'French peasants and farmers were living entirely off the land on vegetables'.

Shortly after the war began the Defence of the Realm Act (DORA) was passed. This was a curtailment of the civil liberties that the government considered necessary in time of war. These included:

- not talking about military or naval matters in public places
- not buying binoculars
- not trespassing on railway lines or bridges
- not lighting bonfires or fireworks
- not ringing church bells
- not being able to buy brandy or whisky in railway refreshment rooms
- not using invisible ink
- not giving bread to horses or chickens
- not melting down any gold or silver

In addition, DORA also gave the government certain powers by which they could:

- try any civilian breaking these laws
- censor newspapers
- take over any factory or workshop
- take over any land
- take any future measures which might be considered necessary in time of war

The intrusion of war regulations on daily life was clearly having an adverse effect among those left at home for drunkenness was becoming a major issue. There was now yet another debate on the question of the national drink problem. Someone in government discovered that the alcohol bill of the country for the last six months of 1915 was greater than it had been in the same period for 1914. This could have been due to a number of causes but to people like David Lloyd George there was only one cause, and that was the tendency of the British public at large to over-indulge itself with alcohol. There were further calls for licensing hours to be restricted, despite protests from licensees, and the Liquor Traffic Control Board decided that a wide-ranging enquiry would be held that should hear from all parties, including the licensees. After all, if the population needed to defend itself against German invasion it would need to be sober to do so. As part of the war economy drive there was also talk of possibly curtailing shop opening hours. There were already shortages of meat and milk and reduced opening hours would help when supplies were restricted. Glossop was not the only place to suffer by any means, but there were arrests for drunkenness on a weekly basis, sometimes even on a daily basis. One Glossop farmer got so drunk on rum that he accused the chief constable of being the kaiser. It was declared nationally that 'drink is the greater enemy at home' and the government reacted sharply. Under their powers conferred by DORA they ordered that beer should be watered down and, under a No Treating Order, that pub customers were not allowed to buy rounds of drinks. Pub opening hours were to be curtailed. Their opening times were reduced from 5am – 12.30am (19½ hours per day) to 12.00 noon – 2.30pm and 6.30pm – 9.30pm (a mere 5½ hours per day). Glossop Licensed Victuallers Association led an angry resistance to this order because it had reduced their ability to trade by almost 75 per cent. While reluctantly accepting some daytime restrictions, they wanted a return to 11pm closing. It was not to be. Excessive drinking had long been a problem and the DORA daytime restrictions on pubs remained in place for well over half a century after the ending of the Great War. Even today, 100 years later, special licences must still be obtained in order to legally sell alcohol after 11pm.

The Battle of Neuve Chapelle in mid-March temporarily raised spirits with a British success, but the British offensive was halted by the Germans soon afterwards. Fighting in the Dardanelles and on the Gallipoli peninsula had been prolonged, intense and bloody on both sides. On 11 May, a temporary armistice was called so that the numbers of dead could be buried. Recruiting pressure was increasing and there were a number of advertisements in the local papers advocating call-up. High Peak Conservatives' political meetings gave way to recruiting meetings and a recruitment campaign was launched in Glossop. Letters home from the Front were still in optimistic tones, although a Cheshire Territorials officer had written in one report, which was published in the *Glossop Chronicle*, that 'casualties are sickening[...]but all the damage is being done by heavy artillery'. However, he fervently believed 'that the War will be over by Christmas and I will be home for my plum pudding'. This was followed by a description of the dreaded Zeppelins and their powers of destruction. The Germans had also begun to use chlorine gas against their enemies and this filled the English troops with 'bitter revengeful feelings against the Germans'. The gas had a devastating effect on the stomach and central nervous system and some soldiers died. Many were affected for life. The death toll among those Glossop men who had enlisted was increasing. But despite this, the Volunteer Movement (known latterly as the Territorials) was growing steadily, although it was said, somewhat unsurprisingly, to be 'in need of spiritual encouragement'.

Partington Convalescent Home, close to the swimming pool at the top of Howard Park, belonging to Glossop Corporation, opened with forty beds at the end of October in 1914 to help cope with the numbers of wounded Belgian refugees who were coming to the town. The hospital came under the Western Command and County of Cheshire, and was affiliated to the Second Western Hospital in Manchester. By spring 1915, Partington, which had just two doctors and was run by its matron, Miss Pepper, could no longer cope alone with the numbers of wounded personnel and Major Hill-Wood, a member of a prominent Glossop family, decided to lend his house, Moorfields, to become a Red Cross hospital. The hospital was administered by Glossop Red Cross and had 102 beds. There were four doctors and a matron, Sister Lovell. Moorfields is a large house and stands outside the town in its own extensive grounds. It proved to be an ideal place, with plenty of bracing fresh air, in which exhausted and wounded soldiers could recover, and there was a good community spirit. There was also an isolation hospital for infectious diseases in the (then) tiny hamlet of Gamesley which adjoined Glossop. But this was used almost exclusively for local townsfolk. Fundraising events were held for both the convalescent home and the military hospital and in early September the whole of the proceeds from the Whitfield well-dressings was donated to be shared between the Partington Home and Moorfields Hospital. Local people donated eggs, fruit, cakes, biscuits, marmalade, flowers, cigarettes and tobacco to both hospitals. As well as Shaw House, there were several wounded Belgian patients at Partington, and Glossop gave generously to the local Belgian relief fund, which totalled £712 14s 8d (just under £25,000). The town also gave generously to the national relief fund for the war and managed to raise £12,656 8s 2d (about £442,690).

The German U-boats campaign to starve the UK meant they were sinking as much merchant shipping as they could. David Lloyd George's

Moorfields, Glossop, c1900, became a military hospital during the Great War

response to this was 'the country must return to old simple living'. Along with the rest of the country, Glossop housewives were told to use as many vegetables as possible and to concentrate on cooking soups and stews while being 'creative but sparing' in their use of flour to make their own bread, cakes, biscuits, pastry, dumplings and pasties, etc. Glossop had been a farming community before the mills transformed the town and a good number of farms still existed. They had their own problems to face, however. A shortage of milking staff, as a result of men enlisting in the army, and the rising price of feeding stuffs led to the dispersal of dairy herds and the practice of selling livestock before it reached maturity. Farmers were instructed that this latter practice was to be stopped and that they must avoid the slaughter of calves and all female-breeding animals. The fat-stock market, the rearing and selling of cattle for meat, was thriving by contrast, especially as meat could now be frozen and stored until required and had provided much-needed extra income. Farmers were told that pigs should be allowed to roam freely and to feed either on grass or on forage crops, not on imported feeds or foods previously considered household waste. In addition, they were also requested to grow more potatoes and root crops, like carrots, parsnips and turnips.

As spring turned to summer, food prices rose steadily. Wheat prices were fixed across the pond in Chicago. A 4lb (1.7kg) loaf of bread cost 10 ½ d (£1.53) and a pound (425 grams) of beef cost 1s 7 ½ d (£2.84). Cold storage facilities were blamed for the high price of bacon as it enabled suppliers to hoard it until prices were forced up. Instead of selling for between 10d (£1.46) and 11d (£1.60) per pound (425 grams), the price rose to 1s 2d (£2.04) or 1s 3d (£2.23) per pound (425 grams). Duty on beer increased so that it was now 3d (£1.05) for a pint (0.57 litres). Glossop townsfolk were feeling the pinch. Men were still enlisting voluntarily but the possibility of compulsory conscription was now being widely discussed. Glossop Trades Council openly condemned this possibility. The town was already suffering enough, they argued, with short-time working, breadwinners signing up and leaving dependent families with little or no means of support, and from a general loss of trade. An attempt to provide a little diversion from the daily hardships was made by 'a photo-drama of creation[...]from the bible to moving pictures', which was being staged at the Victoria Hall in Glossop. One element compared the size of dinosaurs to elephants. The diplodocus was said to have been 'three elephants long and three elephants high', while the gigantosaurus was measured as 160ft (just over 49m) long. However, the number of elephants needed to make this length was not recorded.

On 7 May, the British liner, the *Lusitania*, was sunk 14 miles off the coast of the Irish Republic (at the Old Head of Kinsale) by a German U-boat. There had been nearly 2,000 people on board and of these almost 1,200 died. In an uncomfortable echo of the sinking of the Titanic five years beforehand, the ship sank within eighteen minutes and there was little chance of launching many of the lifeboats properly due to listing. Two young girls from Glossop were on board and were fortunate to be among those who survived and were rescued. Others from nearby towns were not so lucky. Afterwards there was international outrage as it contravened generally accepted war protocols to attack passenger ships not known to be carrying troops or munitions. The Germans insisted that they had fired only one torpedo, but witnesses said that there were two explosions and it was the second explosion that had caused the ship to sink. In 2008, divers discovered around 4,000,000 US Remington .303 bullets in the wreck of the *Lusitania*, which would have been in her cargo. If that was the case then all those aboard the ship were truly victims of the war.

Glossop Football Club finally dropped out of the Second Division in the summer of 1915. Formed in 1886, they had worked their way up to the Second Division by the beginning of the 1898-1899 season. Their crowning achievement was their membership of the First Division for one year in the 1899-1900 season (there was no Premier Division back in those days), when they had won their laurels by being runners up to Manchester City in the Second Division. The club was sponsored by Sir Samuel Hill-Wood, a Glossopian who became the MP for High Peak, the area which included Glossop, from 1910-1929. He also became chairman of Arsenal Football Club in London, beginning an association of the Hill-Wood family with the club that was to last for several decades. The following season, 1900-1901, Glossop finished last in the First Division and were relegated back to the Second Division. The team remained in the Second Division until the end of the 1914-1915 season, when it was felt that there were 'greater and graver matters than sport' and, in any case, there was no money to pay the players. Many clubs revived after the war, but not Glossop. A small non-league team still play at their North End ground, but the glory days are long gone.

Glossop Football Club shared their North End Ground with Glossopdale Cricket Club, formed in 1833, of which Sir Samuel Hill-Wood also became chairman. The legendary W.G. Grace captained a South of England cricket team, which played at Glossop in 1874 against the local team. Needless to say, W.G. Grace and his team won. In 1880 the Manchester Guardian praised the North End ground for its pleasant situation in Glossop, 'an amphitheatre of the hills', but criticised it on two points. 'It adjoins the railway of the Great Central Company[…]the noise is rackety and dreadful and at times the smoke from the engines obscures both hill and valley[...]the other drawback is that the ground is five or six feet higher at one side than the other.' In the years prior to the Great War, Glossop Cricket Club had been a training experience for many Derbyshire CCC cricketers, one of the most famous of whom had been Charles Ollivierre. He played for the West Indies and became the first black West Indian to play county cricket in England. Cricket in Glossop suffered as football had done during the Great War, but friendly matches continued to be played informally, mostly involving the two military hospitals in Glossop, and, after the end of the Great War, Glossopdale Cricket Club recovered in a way that seemed to elude Glossop Football Club.

August saw the first anniversary of the start of the war and there were commemorative church services held in the town. The Germans celebrated by occupying Warsaw. By now it was beginning to dawn in the national consciousness that this war was not going to be over any time soon. It was costing an unprecedented amount, both in human and financial terms. Belgium had been laid waste. There was no employment in that country and millions were starving. France was suffering badly. The UK was struggling. The fighting in the Dardanelles and Gallipoli had taken a terrible toll. William Brocklehurst wrote that 'the economic ravages of war are greater with civilised nations than with barbarians[...]especially through the destruction of the ingenious credit system'. The length of the war, it was said, might be determined by economics as the decisive factor due to the sheer cost of the conflict. There was a heavy burden of taxation placed on the general population to pay for everything, as has been the way throughout history, and it has not changed, the poorer elements in society suffered the most. The Glossop trade unions received a series of blows due to the loss of jobs, loss of manpower, being forced to place unskilled workers in craft tradesmen's posts and, finally, having to accept the employment of women as piecers in the spinning rooms. This last measure caused an outcry and much criticism because of the fight to get girls out of the spinning rooms on health grounds in the latter part of the nineteenth century. However, it was a case of needs must. Piecers' jobs were unsuitable for the older men in the 60-65 age bracket and there were no young lads available. The spinning rooms had to be kept going to produce khaki blankets, flannels, hosiery and uniforms needed by the troops.

In August, National Registration took place in Glossop as everywhere else. This arose from Lord Derby's proposed scheme to get more men to enlist voluntarily in the forces. On 15 August, every adult in the country between the ages of 15 and 65 was required to register to establish their gender, skills and dependants. Men eligible were then 'invited to attest their willingness for military service'. Those who did were grouped according to age, marital status and the type of work they did. However, many men did not attest and some did not even register. There were those who were conscientious objectors and those who felt they could not leave dependent families or sick parents, but there was also another not quite so pleasant element. Some masters and men seized the opportunity to profiteer from the labour shortage, 'greedily grasping after abnormal profits and excessive wages', as the vicar of Hepworth near Holmfirth in West Yorkshire put it. This caused a lot of angst among those who had freely volunteered to enlist to do their patriotic duty and keep England safe. Great exception was taken to the profiteers whose attitude appeared to be that they would enjoy the freedom they had to get rich quick at the expense of those foolish enough to go and fight and possibly get themselves killed. This gave rise to an even more unpleasant phenomenon, that of the White Feather Brigade. In late August a girl named Mary, whose boyfriend was already in khaki, wrote to the *Glossop Chronicle* suggesting that men of military call-up age in civilian dress should be given white feathers by young and attractive girls while they were out on their Sunday walks, and she invited local poultry keepers to send in white feathers for this purpose. Amazingly, many did so. This practice caused a great deal of resentment and hurt and there was fierce opposition to Mary and her kind for, while there were some 'profiteers and shirkers', most of those in civilian clothes had either already served in the army and been invalided out or had been declared medically unfit to serve despite their wish to do so. There were also those

Cavalry non-commissioned officer, c1915.

138

in exempted professions, like munitions workers and uniform supplies manufacturers, who were not allowed by the government to enlist.

In September, the Theatre Royal on Victoria Street closed. The corrugated iron theatre had been set-up and managed by Sydney Spencer and stood on the site of what is now the telephone exchange behind the Town Hall. Spencer had connections and had received good wishes from Henry Irving and Beerbohm Tree when the theatre opened in 1904. One of the highlights was a production of *The Colleen Bawn* at Easter in 1907. Tastes were changing, however, and new moving pictures were rapidly overtaking theatre and music hall in popularity. There had also been competition from the Glossop Empire Theatre on High Street West and the Electric Palace, which had opened in 1911 on George Street (on the site of what is now the medical centre), and which had been refurbished and re-opened on New Year's Day of 1915 by Mr T. Allen-Edwardes. Dysons Dioramas were popular at the theatre. These were elaborate lantern shows mixed with songs performed by a choir. The Electric Palace offered 'refined and tasteful entertainment' and showed a variety of films throughout the war, including Pearl White in *The Clutching Hand*, and stars such as Mary Pickford, Charlie Chaplin, Fatty Arbuckle and Mack Sennett, who was the owner of the Keystone Studios in California. It was an era of 'slapstick, custard pie and wild west', of elaborately over-acted roles and the famously comic antics of the Keystone Cops; the 'hey-day' of the silent film, accompanied by appropriate music usually provided by a cinema in-house piano or organ. Cinemas became places of escape where, just for an hour or two, people could forget the dreadful reality of war.

There was a growing need for increased production of food, supplies for the forces and good economic management. The prime minister, H.H. Asquith, now insisted 'it is necessary to reduce imports and retain exports to fund the War'. This was aimed at abolishing free trade and imposing a 'tariff of import duties' on commodities such as tea to raise funds for the war. The free traders hit back with the accusation that such charges would result in a reduction of the demand for tea, or for other commodities on which they were imposed, and would therefore hurt the trading in parts of the empire, such as India and Ceylon (now Sri Lanka). Asquith was unimpressed. At home he was pleading for luxuries and frivolities to be given up, for civilian clothing to be homemade, for household expenditure to be reduced and the economic cooking of food, and for people to adopt a 'make do and mend policy'. Most Glossopians were already doing much of this anyway and they made further gestures by not booking their usual annual Wakes holidays in resorts such as Blackpool, Morecambe or Southport, and contenting themselves with a day trip to Manchester. Glossop town council, eager to do their bit, decided to make a range of economic savings as well. The Highways and Buildings Department shed ten of their staff and two people at the swimming baths lost their jobs, as well as the head gardener's assistant in Howard Park, which fronted both the swimming pool and Partington Convalescent Home. The isolation hospital lost one of its nurses and the gas meters in the hospital were reduced. The lighting of streetlamps was delayed until 24 September and only alternate lamps were lit. All-night lighting was discontinued, the lamps switched off at 9.45pm. The reading rooms at the free libraries closed at 9pm, presumably to give people time to reach home before the self-imposed curfew due to darkened streets. A few small primary schools were closed and the pupils transferred to other bigger local schools, and some certificated teachers were replaced by un-certificated teachers. Building and sanitary projects were put on hold. Court elections were deferred and overdue rates payments were pursued.

At the end of September, the Battle of Loos took place. It proved to be the largest British offensive of 1915 on the Western Front and was aimed at breaking through German defences in Artois and Champagne. It was also the first time that the British used poison gas in warfare. Despite this, however, lack of ammunition and troops led to a British failure. In mid-October, Bulgaria declared war on Serbia and invaded the country with the result that France and Britain both declared war on Bulgaria in turn. An urgent call for more fighting men went out and, as part of the national recruitment drive, a large recruitment rally took place in early October on Norfolk Square. Major Samuel Hill-Wood and Lieutenant J.B. Martingdale addressed the crowds. There were known to be 3,000 men in Glossop eligible to serve who had not joined-up. This was estimated to be just under a seventh of the total population. Mostly the reason was the problem of leaving their dependants without adequate means of support while a few doubted their own courage. There was, however, great general contempt for those profiteering from the labour shortages. A touch of propaganda was added by the reading of a letter from an un-named soldier in France writing home to say that 'fighting beats football' and that he was 'having a wonderful time in the trenches and would not miss it [the trench warfare]!'. In some cases Glossop fathers and sons were fighting side-by-side in the fierce and prolonged fighting in the Dardanelles (although this had scarcely been reported in Glossop) as

German troops by makeshift shelter in the Forest of Argonne, France, 1915.

well as in France and Belgium. Another spoke of 'the splendid men[...]cheerful and singing as if going to a football match before going to fight the Germans'. There were now weekly casualties from the town being reported at the Front. Most of those serving from Glossop were fighting in France and Belgium. Descriptions of trench warfare had

filtered back but letters from men serving in the forces were heavily censored and even the war correspondents for the press had to accept censorship of their reports so that the true horrors of war were not revealed to those waiting back at home.

Glossop town council pursued its war economies policy vigorously and some of those economies were now biting hard, particularly in the area of sanitation. Unlike many of its more urban neighbours, Glossop still had a basic system of pail closets. The conversions of such closets to the water carriage system, i.e. flushing toilets, was gradually being carried out and 'pails were not being provided in new properties'. In 1914, twenty-eight pail closets had been converted but, due to the war, council building and sanitation works were now suspended. There were still 3,956 pail closets and 163 privy middens in operation throughout Glossop, which meant that about half the town's population lived in homes with pail closets. Ginnels (narrow passages) often ran between the backs of parallel rows of houses for the night waste men. There was a unique 'scavenging system', as it was known, in operation, involving 'the contents of pails emptied into barrels on a weekly or fortnightly basis and then carried down to the Sewage Disposal Works'. This was 'a filthy business', and cost almost as much as 'water closets...which reduce disease'. The whole process was little more than medieval, and the imagination revolts at even thinking about what it entailed, but the practicalities must have made life very uncomfortable in many respects for large numbers of working class people already struggling with difficult working conditions and often inadequate wages.

Hyde and Glossop Weavers Amalgamation, along with the Lancashire Weavers Amalgam, received a 5 per cent war bonus for increased output, but short-time working (35 hours per week) was already in operation at Woods Mills in Howard Town, due to 'bad trade'. A thirty five-hour week is now regarded as normal, but 100 years ago a fifty-five hour week in the mills constituted normal working. The mills had formerly closed only on Saturday afternoons so that workers could play or watch football, and on Sundays. Although Sumners at Wren Nest Mills were back on full-time working, one 'shed' each week had to be stopped because the mules could not be kept running as a result of the labour shortages. Wages might generally have increased by 17 per cent as the war progressed, for those lucky enough to be in work, but there had also been a 35 per cent increase in retail prices. Food prices rose steadily throughout 1915 as a result of the heavy bombardment of merchant shipping. By November, the average 30 shillings (£52.50) weekly shopping basket bill had increased to 42 shillings (£77). Then Sumners decided to stop the allowances scale due to altered conditions for men enlisting, although they promised that the existing allowances for dependants of fighting men would continue and that they would try and give jobs back to these serving military personnel after the war. The recruitment campaign was increasing in Glossop. Members of the local police force put themselves forward to sign-up and all the staff at Glossop railway station also volunteered. Classes began in Manchester for training females as clerks so they could work in offices and several Glossop women attended these classes. There was much male grumbling about mere women doing such work, but essential services needed to be maintained and women were keen to do their bit as well as men. Pensioners were also having a seriously bad time of it. Their weekly pension amounted to just 5 shillings (£8.75) each week and unless they lived with family members it was almost impossible to survive. There was always the option of the workhouse in Old Glossop, but that was an option that most tried to avoid.

An unexpected side effect of the war was the war weddings rush. The number of marriages, both locally and nationally, increased dramatically. There was a very real fear that many of the men might not come back and couples feared losing out on what might be their only chance to get married and share some sort of life together, however brief. 'Pretty weddings' were reported every week by the *Glossop Chronicle*, a welcome antidote to the rest of the news, which was grim enough, and the constant stream of war casualties. Weddings were a much simpler affair than today. Better-off girls might wear a long white dress, but many working-class girls from the town just chose a pretty dress, often in shades of blue or cream, which they could wear time and again. Such dresses were frequently made by either the girl or a member of her family and accessorised with a hat and bunches of in-season flowers. A mother or grandmother might lend a treasured brooch or necklace for her to wear on the big day. The traditional adage, for weddings, of the bride wearing 'something old, something new, something borrowed, something blue' could have come from this era. The 'wedding breakfast' for many brides would be just a home-made wedding cake and a cup of tea or a sit-down meal at the girl's home for immediate family, the bridesmaids and best man. Often there was neither the money nor the time for a honeymoon but the luckier ones might afford one night in a cheap Manchester hotel. When Annie Turner married Charles Goddard in a pretty wedding at All Saints Parish Church in Glossop three weeks before Christmas she wore a 'navy blue satin robe with a matching hat, and carried a bouquet of white chrysanthemums and red roses', all the colours of the national flag. It was the bridesmaids who wore simple white dresses. Afterwards tea was served in Woods Reading Rooms and then the wedding party made their own entertainment with music and dancing.

At the end of November the Serbian Army collapsed and retreated to the Adriatic coast from where it was eventually evacuated by the French and Italian navies. The Allies had lost one of their number and the outlook was grim. 'The War must be won by money as well as men and munitions because it is only by money that men and munitions can be kept going,' thundered one politician. But although there were hints in the Glossop papers for Christmas shopping, many Glossopians didn't have much heart for it even if they had spare cash. Any cash they did have they gave to Christmas parcel funds for the troops. The mayoress reported that her Christmas fund had received 'an excellent response'. There were several Christmas events, parties and festivities staged, but all of them were focussed on treats for the forces. Families were asked not to send perishable goods as there might be time delays in delivery, during which certain foodstuffs, like fresh fruit or vegetables, butter, bacon, bread or cheese, might spoil. Fruitcakes, biscuits, tinned food, bottles of spirits, 'baccy' or cigarettes, maybe something warm and dry to wear, were all recommended and very welcome to their recipients. There had been a description that had somehow avoided the censors, of life in water-filled trenches, the cold, the discomfort, the relentlessness of it all, published in the *Glossop Chronicle,* which must have horrified those who had loved ones serving abroad. Certainly those troops from Glossop were vociferous in their 'warm appreciation' and thank you letters for the Christmas gifts and food parcels sent from the town, although it was little enough to relieve the nightmare in which they found themselves.

Hawkshead Mill, Glossop, which became a munitions factory in the Great War. The roll of honour is just visible on the end wall.

Chapter Three

1916

SOME CHRISTMAS AND New Year parties were held in Glossop but always with one thought in mind: the troops on active service. The mayor started a project for collecting books and magazines to be sent to all soldiers and sailors. Waste newspapers were collected for the national fund. A patriotic wool fund was started in the town. Local sewing circles produced socks, gloves, flannels and nightwear to be sent to soldiers at the Front. The sewing circles named after the mayoress and the late Mrs Anne Kershaw-Wood seemed to be two of the largest and most productive. In September 1915, the Women's Institute formed its first branch in Wales with the aim of encouraging women to help increase food production. In Glossop, during the teens and twenties, the sewing circles fulfilled both a practical and social function, and when local women did become involved in helping food production it was through growing vegetables in their gardens or working on allotments, individually, and not as part of a group. Perhaps as encouragement, or just demonstrating how women could do their bit, the *Glossop Chronicle* printed a short piece about a Bulgarian peasant lady, aged 132, who had spent her whole life in her own village and who had spent over a century working in the fields. She was born in May 1784, and a local monastery had kept her baptism certificate. In January 1916 she was still alive but had, not surprisingly, retired from field work.

Casualties were growing and Glossop was losing men on a weekly basis. In Kent seven brothers from one family had been killed in the war. Letters of grateful thanks arrived from men in the trenches, heavily censored, but glimpses of their unenviable lifestyle crept though. One young soldier wrote that some of the troops were up to their knees in mud and water and others were waist deep in water. He himself 'regularly puddled through mud[...]and only had a bit of jam and cheese for a Christmas treat before the parcels arrived'. This supported statements in the national press to the effect that 'troops are ill equipped[...]through hopeless forgetfulness on the part of the authorities'. In early January the Gallipoli Campaign had ended in defeat for the Allies and a victory for the Ottoman Empire. It was a humiliating experience for all those on the Allied side who had fought so gallantly. It was, therefore, hardly surprising that recruitment numbers were faltering. There was also great and sometimes heated debate over the principle that single men should volunteer before married men. Those who were married felt they had responsibilities for dependants and should not be the first to go. Single men felt they were being unfairly targeted and that enlisting should be across the board for all those of military age, i.e. 19-40. Lord Kitchener's initial appeal for troops followed by Lord Derby's scheme for attestation had been reasonably successful in Glossop, but many other towns had not shown the same enthusiasm. There might have been no need for compulsory conscription but there were still large numbers of young men who had not attested and voluntary enlistment was not attracting the numbers of recruits needed to replace the heavy losses among fighting men. David Lloyd George had realised this for some time and so, on 27 January, the Military Service Act was passed. The passing of the Compulsory Conscription Act was big news and widely debated. Men would now be forced to enlist and fight unless exempted by age, medical fitness, or they were working in a starred occupation deemed essential for the war.

It was the first time that military conscription had been introduced and all unmarried men between 18-41 were liable to be called-up unless they were already serving in the navy. In May, this was extended to married men as well. Enlistment for immediate service had dropped, due in no small part to the raging debate of whether single men should go before married men. But there had been busy scenes at the attesting stations and khaki armlets were given out to verify that a man had attested. There were forty-six groups under the Lord Derby scheme. Single men were grouped according to age in the first twenty-three groups. Married men were grouped the same way into the remaining forty-three groups. Medical examinations were given to the men awaiting call-up at that point. Wearers of attestation armlets were told to always carry Army Form W394 with them in case they were challenged by an officer, an NCO or the police. Enlisting men were also told that they must shave off their beards, although they could retain close shaved moustaches, the reason given being that, as Alexander the Great had discovered over 2,000 years before, the enemy could grab soldiers by their facial hair and inflict horrendous injuries upon them. The town, for the moment, was focused on the call-up question and the heavy losses the local 6th Cheshire Regiment was suffering. The army realised too late the dangers of Pals or Mates battalions in that it often meant the deaths of a number of men from just one or two streets. All the men who had attested under the Derby Scheme during National Registration were now being called-up and, on 20 January, the groups two, three, four and five of the Derby recruits were called-up. Any claims for postponement or exemption, which was usually limited to six months, had to be made within ten days. A few days later groups six, seven, eight and nine, single men aged 23-27 years old, were called-up. Almost unbelievably, at the same time there was also a plea for an increase in the birth rate as 'compensation for war wastage'. Quite how the women were going to achieve this while their men were serving abroad, and they were living in greatly reduced circumstances was not explained. The White Feather Brigade was still active and causing such grief that khaki armlets were now being supplied to men not in uniform who were on leave or convalescing on production of their army card.

The cotton trade was suffering badly due to a scarcity of male labour. In Glossop there was a number of appeals made by individuals and employers for exemption of some workers from military service, but most of these were refused. Wages were not keeping pace with inflation and rising prices. Greenfield and Waterside Mills were given over to the manufacture of munitions instead of cotton, and Hawkshead Mill in Old Glossop, owned by Isaac Jackson, also began the manufacture of munitions. The old mill buildings still stand and there is a roll of honour on the end wall commemorating those employees from the mill who fought for their country but did not return. There were those who had believed that the linen famine would encourage the cotton industry, but this proved not to be so. Flax, used for the manufacture of linen, now cost £200 (nearly £6,000) per ton as opposed to £80 (just under £2,400) before the war. However, cotton was also in short supply due to the constant German bombardment of British shipping and the reluctance at government level to seek alternative supply sources for cotton. So the industry was unable to benefit from extra trading opportunities. Despite the privations, workers in the Glossop cotton trade still agreed to help fund three motor ambulances for the use of sick and wounded soldiers on the French and Belgian Fronts.

By the end of January the effects of war were biting hard. Manchester and District, of which Glossop was on the perimeter, were using 3,000 tons of sugar per week. Most sugar was still imported. It was essential that demand for this be reduced and, consequently, there was a sugar shortage. Butter production in the north-west was also declining as

Roll of honour at Hawkshead Mill, c1918, in tribute to those from the mill who died in the Great War.

Cheshire farmers were switching to cheese production because of its greater profitability. Milk prices rose due to reduced output despite the introduction of female milking staff, and the use of what many termed new-fangled machines. There was great resistance from farmers towards both machinery and employing women to milk the cows. While there was no doubt a Luddite element in the suspicion of machines doing the work of men, or women, the tradition of English milkmaids and dairy maids was centuries old and, if anything, it was surprising that this had become a male-orientated domain. Lighting in the Borough of Glossop was further restricted in case of Zeppelin raids and, much to the horror of some locals, female lamplighters were employed. Libraries closed at 7pm while shops, churches, public halls and all households were to have dark coloured blinds. Lloyd George had condemned many British working men as 'drunken shirkers', so, under the Defence of the Realm Act, all pubs and off-licences were now restricted to just five-and-a-half hours opening on weekdays. There were fifty-nine pubs and seventeen off-licences in Glossop and not one was granted any exemption. Alcohol was not to be sold from any 'van, barrow or basket' in the street either, and spirits were to be diluted with water so they were no more than 50 per cent proof. This resulted in a big decrease in drunkenness and drunken offences, certainly in Glossop where the drunken offenders had all been men.

It was a hard winter in Glossop in 1916. There were 30-foot-deep snowdrifts in the Peak District, and Snake Pass, which runs from Glossop to Sheffield, was blocked for a month. People shivered and tried to keep warm as best they could. Farmers lost livestock, mostly sheep, in the snow. The army bought up all straw stocks to feed their war horses. Local cotton workers were still pressing for higher wages to cope with steadily rising costs and were threatening to strike because wages were not keeping pace with inflation. Soldiers from Glossop at the Front read the *Glossop Chronicle*, which was sent to them by families and friends, and some wrote to the paper regularly. The cotton wages dispute caused great resentment amongst them. It wasn't so much that they could not sympathise but more the feeling that they were risking death every day to keep their country safe, earning a comparative pittance, while other folk seemed to be squabbling over who got what. Of course it was not that simple, but to the men standing cold and wet, knee-deep in water in muddy trenches with German bullets flying over their heads, a strike for higher wages by those safe at home didn't exactly rate as a matter of the gravest importance. It was a similar reaction to that caused by the business of conscientious objectors. Soldiers were dying to allow others the freedom to believe and to act according to their beliefs. It all seemed to be a bit one-sided and this feeling intensified as they buried yet more of their colleagues who had been shot dead by German snipers or blown to pieces by shells. Although the *Glossop Chronicle* faithfully reported all deaths of local military personnel the words 'killed in action' or 'he died a hero' euphemistically masked the bloody and filthy reality which the soldiers faced every day.

Flour and sugar prices were still rising and there seemed to be a general shortage of meat and sugar. The drive to make lump sugar a luxury was not succeeding and customers still demanded lump, crystals or granulated in equal quantities. Sugar rationing was both feared and expected for the world supply of sugar had decreased by 2,000,000 tons as a result of the war. The price of butter and cheese had also risen, as there were now no Irish supplies. There were taxes on tea, coffee and cocoa. The latter now cost four times what it had pre-war. There was a new tax placed on matches, both safety and ordinary, and also on all entertainments. Surprisingly the tax on entertainments did not cause much fuss, perhaps because, unlike food, it was not a necessity of life. Easter was not celebrated until late April in 1916, and the services held in Glossop churches tried to be optimistic. On Easter Monday, 24 April, an Easter Rising by the Irish Republicans was mounted in Dublin. Their aim was to end British rule in Ireland. The British Army in Ireland quickly suppressed the rebellion, but it all detracted from what should have been a united front against a common enemy. The *Glossop Chronicle* didn't inform its readers what had taken place. There was praise for the local volunteers movement and further appeals were made for the Glossop Belgian relief fund. Reports had appeared in national papers about the First Battle of Liege and night trench digging in Flanders, and somehow seemed to convey a promise that maybe the war would soon be over. Despite this there were several Zeppelin attacks in Lancashire and folk watched the skies nervously for the huge, well-lit airships, which could inflict such destruction.

Heavy casualties among Glossop men were listed in May and June and the recruitment campaign moved up a gear. The father of one local 'shirker', as he labelled his son who had applied again for exemption from fighting, publicly determined that the boy 'would do the manly thing and go to war'. However, in May, all of this was overshadowed by the death of the much loved mayor of Glossop, Herbert Partington JP. Tributes poured in and the latest war casualties shared column-inch space in the newspaper with an obituary and remembrances of Mr Partington. There was a lot of public grief and finally his wife, the lady mayoress, agreed to take over as mayor in his place. A lady mayor was another first for the town but, like her husband, she was popular and well-loved, and, by filling her husband's shoes she gave the town some sense of continuity and security.

Rising food prices were a constant problem and claims for increased allowances and financial help were common. A typical weekly shopping list for an adult and child for a week who were living on the separation allowance of 17s 6d (approximately £26.25) is given below:

bread	1s	6 ½ d
milk	1s	6d
sausages		9d
rabbit	1s	6d
¼lb tea		7d
½cwt coal		8 ½ d
4 meat faggots		4d
margarine		5d
sugar		9d
1lb bacon	1s	2d
oats		5d
beans		1 ½ d
marmalade		3 ½ d
2oz cocoa		2 ½ d
potatoes/greens		6 ½ d
2 packets soup		4d
½lb cheese		6d
laundry		7d
soap, matches		3d
Total		17s 2d (around £26)

This did not include any money for gas, clothing, tram fares or treats for the child.

Trying to think of ways to save on fuel, lighting and black-outs, the government came up with a new Daylight Saving Act under the powers invested in them by the Defence of the Realm Act. It came into force on 21 May 1916. The clocks were to go forward by one hour and would remain so until around the end of September, when the days started to draw in and the clocks would be put back an hour. Putting the clocks on

Market and Town Hall commemoration plaque of Mr and Mrs Isaac Jackson's gift to Glossop in 1918, in memory of Glossop soldiers who died in the Great War.

by an hour was no problem but, unfortunately, clocks at that time had no reverse winding mechanism so laborious instructions were issued about winding them forward eleven hours when it was time to go back an hour. The twenty-four-hour clock was not in use, so all clock faces were simply numbered 1-12, which made the process and principles a little easier. British Summer Time (BST) is now standard practice, but this was the first time it had ever been done. There were additional questions about lighting at the important annual Glossop May fair, and more restrictions on public lighting, and a few grumbled. But it was generally accepted by most Glossop folk who recognised the danger of attack from the air.

During the summer months, further restrictions gradually tightened their hold on Glossop. House repairs and maintenance were suffering because of the lack of skilled tradesmen. There was still the question of the pail closets and scavenging system. Together with the loss of general maintenance, this caused hygiene problems, especially where there was a lack of light and ventilation, which was a particular problem with the back-to-back style of house building. Infant mortality rose and so too did the incidence of tuberculosis, better known as consumption. The problems of milk production seemed to increase with farmers receiving little reward for their efforts. In early June Lord Kitchener died. He was drowned when a German U-boat torpedoed the destroyer HMS *Hampshire*, on which he was sailing, off the Orkney Islands. Flags were flown at half-mast over Glossop Town Hall as well as the Moorfields and Partington hospitals. A house-to-house collection for the national children's orphanage also took place around the same time and hard-pressed townsfolk put their hands into their often nearly empty pockets yet once more. This was swiftly followed by a further appeal for the Glossop Belgian relief fund. The number of war casualties was increasing and the need to replace them was becoming ever more urgent. All the talk was of national conscription following the passing of the Act, legalising compulsory call-up and, despite reassurance from the generals commanding the troops, the war did not look as though it was going to end any time soon. There were claims and appeals but not many were granted. The Pelham Committee had issued a list of certain occupations it considered should be exempt from call-up service:

Agriculture
>   farm labourer
>   market gardening
>   fruit growing
>   seed raising
>   making and repairing agricultural machinery
>   agricultural education and organisation

Forestry
> cutting of timber
> hauling of timber
> preparing of timber

Shipping
> mercantile marine
> shipbuilding and ship repairing

Transport
> railways
> canals
> docks and wharves
> cartage connected with docks and wharves

Public utility services
> sanitary services (local authorities)
> fire brigade
> civil hospitals
> workhouses
> infirmaries
> asylums

Red Cross and general welfare
> in camps
> in munitions factories
> in internment camps

Cotton industry
> minders
> piecers
> twiner doublers

Munitions
> all workers engaged in the manufacture of munitions

Glossop had numbers of people engaged in agriculture, the cotton trade and munitions work, but most of that work could be done by women and it was of paramount importance to replenish the numbers of fighting men. If a man was judged to be medically fit it was almost certain that he would see military action at some point. Appeals tribunals dealt with a number of claims for exemption from men who either had a number of people dependent on them and who would suffer real hardship if they enlisted, or from men running small businesses that they would lose if they were called-up. Many appeals were dismissed. The tribunals were not unsympathetic but decided that everyone should have to make some kind of sacrifice for the war and exemptions were only granted on the understanding that the individual found work in one of the exempted occupations for three days each week. Conscientious objectors were a bit harder to deal with, especially if they refused to be flexible on certain points. Most were given the choice of finding full-time employment in an exempted occupation within ten days or they would be ordered to sign-up although they would go on non-combative duties only. Many conscientious objectors accepted this but there were those who refused and they faced arrest and punishment.

People tried to focus on the forthcoming Glossop church festivals and the Corpus Christi procession by St Mary's Roman Catholic church as something to which they could look forward and enjoy. And then the cruellest blow of all was struck. The Battle of the Somme, which took place on 1 July 1916, was a turning point in the Great War. It was meant to be a turning point towards ending the war. Instead it became a turning point for loss of life and morale. General Sir Douglas Haig had taken over command of the troops after Lord Kitchener's death. The attack and the battle were meant to last one day. Instead hostilities lasted 141 days until well into November. Many soldiers in the British Army were inexperienced, being mainly those who had responded to Kitchener's call to arms. Nevertheless, the modus operandi of sending British troops charging over the top was nothing short of suicidal. Eye-witness accounts vary but what cannot be ignored is hard evidence. Certain of victory, Haig requested cameras to film the battle, which took place on 1 July. The film has survived showing just what the troops faced. On that day alone over 19,000 British soldiers were killed and 38,000 wounded. Much has been written about the Somme, both positive and negative but, by the end, Britain had suffered a total of 500,000 casualties, of whom 100,000 died, to gain just 6 miles of territory. At least sixty of them came from Glossop. They included Private Frank Wharmby, the son of local Alderman Wharmby, Private William Bramwell, who helped dig tanks out of the mud on the Somme, and Captain David Cuthbert, who died on the first day of the four-month-long battle. David Cuthbert had formerly been the manager of the

Manchester branch of the British Crown Assurance Society. He was just 30 years old and was said to have 'a fine baritone voice'. His death on the Somme devastated his wife and two young children, aged 4 and 2½, especially as his body was never recovered. Although the number of reported war casualties from Glossop rose sharply in July and early August, the Battle of the Somme scarcely merited a mention in the *Glossop Chronicle*, despite the death of Captain Cuthbert, the most senior officer from Glossop to die in battle. The Somme was also the very first time that the British used armoured tanks, which they did at the Battle of Flers-Courcelette that began on 15 September.

Reporting the Battle of the Somme may have been played down because the military authorities were seriously worried that, if the full truth were known, panic might ensue and morale at home would collapse completely, badly affecting both the war effort and the willingness of men to fight. Morale among troops was already low and this was reflected by the war poets who, prior to the Somme, had written of the glory of war and fighting for what was right, and who were now bitterly disillusioned and wrote of the futility of all the killing and destruction in the mud and blood of the French and Belgian battlefields.

There were more pleas for everyone to help with the war effort in some way and to economise wherever they could, such as not stockpiling food or buying new clothes. Glossop Weavers Association sent parcels to its wounded members containing treats worth about 10 shillings (around £15). One young Glossop soldier, taken prisoner-of-war, wrote to say he was being reasonably treated but pleading for food parcels and cigarettes as the Germans were intending to make him work hard harvesting corn for them. Various suggestions were made to encourage patriotism in the local schools and there was an appeal from the War Office for recruits to undertake special duties, such as joining the volunteer force, becoming special constables or working on munitions. In early August an Ottoman attack on the British in the Sinai peninsula was repulsed. It was a small victory but it was a victory.

There were no cheap rail fares for Glossop Wakes (19-25 August). In any case, the Wakes were becoming a low-key affair since people had little spare cash and less inclination to celebrate with the growing numbers of casualties. Some felt guilty enjoying any fun or entertainment while their loved ones were either risking or losing their lives daily. Whitfield well-dressing went ahead, however, and many people contented themselves by supporting and attending that event. This year the theme was the war and the backdrop of the well-dressing was a large board through which two imitation big guns projected and the slogan 'God Save the King and Empire'. To the side a large arch board proclaimed 'For Our Wounded Soldiers', and it was blessed by the local clergy amid fervent prayers that this dreadful war would soon be ended.

Glossop and Hadfield Weavers Associations were becoming increasingly concerned about high food prices and the steadily rising costs of living. Four-loom weavers had seen their wages drop by nearly a third in real terms since the war began. They were also worried about the problems of pensions being paid to wounded or gassed servicemen who had formerly worked in the industry. Supplementary pensions and separation allowances had become a problem for most Glossop textile manufacturing employers, none of whom had expected the war to last so long. And in mid-September a Glossop War Pensions Committee was set up to try and address these problems. By mid-October, however, the weavers gave up any pretence about just concern over steadily rising food prices and demanded wage rises. By contrast, Glossop Bleachers and Dyers reported reasonable trade but were bitterly resentful of married men being taken to join the forces. The cotton trade in general, though, was beginning to suffer badly from wages falling in value and high prices for foodstuffs. Finally, despite giving an undertaking not to strike during the war, all the carders, seeing their earning potential steadily decreasing, decided to do just that.

The cotton workers were not the only ones to be concerned with pay, or rather the lack of it. In early May, the *Glossop Chronicle* ran a blistering attack on what it termed 'a burning injustice'. Soldiers' pay was worse than inadequate and the munitions workers, safe at home in the mother country, could earn four- to five-times as much as a soldier fighting at the Front. Examples were quoted of soldiers who had been in the army for eight months yet had barely drawn £8 (£240) in pay. Those who were discharged from the army on medical grounds were required to pay the army £4 (around £120) and received regular demand notes for this sum even if they were lying in a hospital bed. Deductions were also made irregularly from army pay for sundry reasons and soldiers never knew how much they would get paid. Even with the separation allowances their families received, the high price of food and fuel made life hard at best. The soldiers could not, of course, protest at this treatment by going on strike and representations were made to the local MP, Major Hill-Wood, to request the House of Commons to end the practices of wildfire deductions and payments made by soldiers on discharge. The rhetoric of the *Glossop Chronicle* almost equalled that of that well-known thunderer *The Times*, as it called 'for justice for the lads in khaki and blue'.

Farming was supposed to be an exempt occupation but now absolutely all men between the ages of 18-41 were needed to join the forces. There was a farm training scheme for women in Yorkshire, but a number of women in the Glossop and Hadfield areas had been brought up on farms and already knew the basic procedures. There was also an unlooked for complication in working on farms that could prove difficult, possibly even dangerous, particularly for female workers. Conscientious objectors were hiding out in huts, barns and tents on some of the more remote farms. There was an increasing and festering resentment towards pacifists and conscientious objectors and it was feared that discovery of these people's hiding places could lead to violence. They had to feed themselves somehow and helping themselves to farm produce was one way of doing it. There was also growing pressure to utilise all available land for growing crops of some description and Glossop council was given powers to rent land from owners and to re-let this land as allotments so there was more opportunity for cultivation. Regulations for commandeered land were strict. It was to be used for annual crops only. No perennial crops were allowed and there was to be no grazing of livestock either.

As the gloom of the shorter days of autumn increased, so too did the gloom caused by yet more restrictions. Milk prices were still rising. So too was the price of cows, and beef was expensive. Sweets were now rationed. There was no more white bread or white flour available. Economy in using potatoes was strongly advised. Glossop suffered along with the rest of the country. Food tickets were soon to be issued to try and ensure that everyone got a share in what basic foodstuffs were available. Imports of dried and tinned fruits, timber, hardware, paper and musical instruments were restricted. Rail fares for 1917 were to increase by 50 per cent. According to their local association, hairdressers in the town were having a hard time as well. Although a haircut cost only four pence (£1.20) and a shave just two pence (60 pence) there were no longer the numbers of men around to take advantage and those who were around often couldn't afford it. Curfews increased. The libraries closed at dusk. Pedestrians stumbled around in the darkened streets, trying to keep to the rule of walking on the right, and there were numerous accidents, mostly caused by people falling off the kerbs. Glossop workers protested at the enforced gloom of the streets. The lists of casualties from the Front seemed to be never-ending. There was a case of typhoid fever reported at Moorfields Military Hospital.

In early December, Henry Asquith resigned as prime minister and was succeeded by David Lloyd George. Christmas fundraising for the troops took place in Glossop as usual and people gave as generously as they could. The mayoress was in overall charge of the distribution of Christmas treats and gifts to those serving abroad. A million eggs were collected every week for the wounded in English hospitals. By this time eggs cost 4s 6d a dozen (just under £7) and were fast becoming a luxury. This was the third Christmas of the war and preparations were muted rather than it being a joyous time of anticipation with family and friends gathered around. There still seemed to be no end in sight to the war and people were not inclined to celebrate. However, many worked hard to ensure that the inmates in the two military hospitals of Moorfields and Partington had a good Christmas. After what the wounded soldiers had suffered, people felt that giving them a decent Christmas was the least they could do.

It was a cold Christmastime in Glossop with 'snow and snow broth', and the 'Peakland hills were garbed in the fleecy element'. The *Glossop Chronicle* published an end-of-year review, which was mostly about the war and its effects, progress, casualties, hardships, shortages, restrictions, etc. National debates on food shortages, war pension payments and the possibility of votes for women were reported, but the Irish question was not mentioned, despite the fact that the Germans had tried to support it. Nor was the assassination on 29 December of Grigori Rasputin, who was very close (some said too close) to both the tsar and tsarina of Russia.

It was a bleak time for all concerned.

Chapter Four

1917

AT NEW YEAR the Glossop churches held Watchnight services. These started late on New Year's Eve and finished in the early hours of New Year's Day. During the services, Christians reviewed the year that had just passed and prayed for the year ahead. It was a muted affair as 1916 had been a grim year and, despite hopes for a better year in 1917, many feared it would bring little joy or comfort.

The mayoress received a large batch of letters from Glossop men serving in Europe full of warm thanks to the givers and workers at home for their Christmas parcels. Some wrote of the dreadful weather conditions at the Front and expressed a hope that 'Christmas 1917 would be the last Christmas of this terrible war'. A bleak poem, called *A Night on the Somme*, echoed these sentiments. There were the usual lists of war casualties, which made grim reading and, although reports of military action tried to sound optimistic, nobody was fooled. In mid January a book written by Arthur Mee and Dr Stuart Holden was published by Morgan and Scott. The title was simply *Defeat!* Although fiercely patriotic it was full of unpalatable facts, such as 10 per cent of the manpower for the war had been wasted and that 10 per cent of the war bill had been wasted. Full of phrases like 'ring and string', and putting forward arguments for prohibition, it claimed that Britain had 'not yet deserved to win the War'.

French agriculture had suffered badly and there was scarcely enough food to feed the French let alone for the troops or for export. There was now an appeal to Derbyshire women to work the land, as women were doing in France and Belgium. All classes of women were encouraged to assist for patriotic reasons, and farmers were instructed that they should not object to female workers. There had been heavy snow storms in the Peak District and many of the farmers were, in any case, heavily occupied by digging out their sheep from snowdrifts. At the end of January a mass meeting was held at Woolley Bridge on the outskirts of Glossop about food shortages, food hoarding, profiteering and the fact that many were going without sufficient food. Children's growth was in danger of being stunted by inadequate nutrition and there were calls for regulation and for a food controller to be appointed. Following this meeting, dairy farmers in the Glossop area offered 100 acres of grazing land to be ploughed for growing food and, in recognition of their gesture, Lord Howard, who owned most of Glossop at the time, said he would pay for re-seeding when the land came to be re-instated as pasture. Seed potatoes were to be purchased for the national food supply, whose rallying cry was 'Food! Organisation! Victory!', and Isaac Jackson, who owned Hawkshead Mills in Old Glossop, offered to pay for Glossop's share of seed potatoes.

Meanwhile there was, quite literally, 'trouble at mill'. Cotton spinners throughout Lancashire, Manchester and the Glossop district had turned down a 10 per cent pay rise and were threatening to strike. The problem was the constant disparity between their wages and the ever-rising prices of food and fuel. Since a stoppage was out of the question, the government threatened to intervene to force them to carry on working. The cotton workers' subsequent request for a 20 per cent advance of wages was also turned down. There was additional trouble at Wren Nest Mills, on the High street in Glossop, where there was disparity in the wages of weavers, with some working between six and eight looms earning nearly twice as much as those working five or six looms. Then there was a disastrous fire at Howard Town Mills in the centre of town, which destroyed all the spinning departments. A few weeks later there was a winders' strike at Woods Mills in Howard Town. The winders wanted more money for their increased workloads. It also didn't help that India had decided to raise war funds by increasing import duty on Lancashire cotton goods from 3.5 per cent to 7.5 per cent. No one could deny that the cotton workers were having a bad time, but nevertheless their actions, compared with those of the men at the Front who fought for their country in conditions that were beyond appalling and who earned far less than the cotton workers, seemed to verge on the insular and self-serving. They were genuinely concerned for their families' welfare. No one could deny that, but it was felt in certain quarters, particularly by some of those serving at the Front, that to do their bit at home and support the troops they should perhaps just shut up and put up. It was an insoluble problem. Fear, hunger and deprivation can easily overcome reason and rationale.

Fundraising for the war was still going on. Farmers gave sheep to be auctioned by the Red Cross. A war sewing circle began meetings in Hadfield. Local voluntary sewing circles sent seventy mufflers, eighty pairs of mittens and fifty-five pairs of socks to troops at the Front. The National Egg Collection for the Wounded, whose patron was Queen

Alexandra, benefitted from donations given by Glossop farms. The official war loan business was conducted by the Post Office. Glossop Corporation invested £2,000 (nearly £50,000) and Glossop Rural District Council invested £500 (almost £12,500). There was also a 'When the Boys Come Home' fund set-up for those who left jobs and homes in Glossop to enlist. National service call-ups were intensifying and teachers were now asked to volunteer help. Employment exchange officials were told to ascertain the most suitable occupations for volunteers. However, the major voluntary effort was now being directed towards 'grow your own'. The Duke of Devonshire was providing free allotments for people to grow food for the war effort and Lord Howard, who owned all the Glossopdale estate, was urged to reduce his allotment rents by 80 per cent from 5/- (£10.25) to 1/- (£2.05). He declined, on the grounds that the allotment charge was to cover fencing, draining and administrative matters, but he did offer to donate a bag of free seed potatoes to his allotment workers.

Glossop allotment workers at Bridgefield started growing potatoes for the national cause. All local elementary schools were to have kitchen gardens where the children would help to grow food for the country. There was garden planting of rhubarb, spring cabbages, peas, celery and parsley. Allotment holders grew carrots, parsnips and onions as well as potatoes. Ludworth farmers were initially opposed towards turning grazing and pasture land for cows into allotments for growing potatoes, but the matter was eventually taken out of their hands by Glossop Rural District Council, on the grounds of the local and national need for food. Lord Howard agreed to accept greatly reduced rent for land on which allotment growers were growing food for the country. Local ploughmen came out of retirement to plough new land for the planting of crops, but there were insufficient numbers for the spring sowings and ploughmen were returned from the Front to help. The Women's Land Army was officially set-up and selection, training and placements were organised. Despite the local acidic soils, the allotments programme was going well and gathering strength, although there was some shortage of seed potatoes. The local Glossop paper was full of gardening hints. In 1917, one lady in Dorset, with just the help of two small boys, produced from her allotment:

sixty bundles of asparagus
fifty bundles of rhubarb
80lb tomatoes
600 lettuces
ten bushels of spinach
twenty bushels of onions
2cwt carrots
2cwt parsnips

Farms in Glossop township of Simmondley. There was also opencast coal mining here. c1920.

three bushels of artichokes
120lb peas
210lb runner beans
two sacks of broad beans
ten bushels of beetroot
210 vegetable marrows
thirty cucumbers
3¼ tons of potatoes

Glossop soils, being more acidic in nature than those of the West Country, and the climate generally being harsher, this sort of abundant output was never going to happen in or around the town, but local farmers and gardeners did their best. Potatoes and onions, beans, celery and rhubarb were quite successful and some other crops did well enough.

Meanwhile, the government was urging more food economy measures. A new loaf was introduced, which included rice, barley, maize, semolina, oats, rye or beans. These additions made the bread darker and more satisfying, although it was of less nutritional value. Rice, haricot beans and pearl barley were to be served as vegetables or used to thicken stews, and housewives were urged to serve oatmeal porridge for breakfast. The *Glossop Chronicle* even went so far as to publish a recipe for scones made from cold fried porridge. The paper could not hide, however, the resigned acceptance and the dull lack of enthusiasm for these latest measures. The war had been dragging on for nearly three long years and folk could see no end to it. Glossopians watched the casualty list of their loved ones grow longer and tried to be stoical, praising the heroism and selflessness of those who had been killed or injured in the fighting, but they couldn't avoid the feeling that so much sacrifice seemed to be made in vain. The *Chronicle* was now publishing weekly war reports, although often in retrospect. After the appalling four-month-long Battle of the Somme, which was supposed to have lasted just one day, incidents like the Dardanelles muddle, where there had been serious, and sometimes fatal, delays in supplying the military forces, mainly owing to administrative incompetence, caused apprehension and despair, especially as the manpower shortage was now critical.

Neville Chamberlain's national service campaign was met with caution. Its aims, of the provision and manufacture of food and munitions together with nursing, driving, clerical services and back-up facilities for the troops, was laudable enough, but there were worries about pay and conditions, promotions and position by those who might apply. It was announced at the end of March that women were to be sent to France for the first time to fill clerical posts, to work as cooks, waitresses, domestic staff, and to act as clerks, telephonists, postal workers and drivers, in order to free up the men so that they could be sent to fight at the Front. Chamberlain made a plea for another 500,000 volunteers for national service but got less than half that number, and of these half were already engaged in essential work. A large body of men was needed to work in agriculture, mines, shipbuilding and munitions to replace the young fit men who were being taken for the army. In addition, despite the newly formed Women's Land Army, ploughmen were still being repatriated from the trenches to help plough for the spring sowings of 1917, and this was causing problems. National service recruits were to be mainly from the 41-61 age group and would be paid 25/- (about £30) per week. The unions were furious about the scheme, seeing it simply as tied labour, while employers used it as a threat against anyone who was a troublemaker.

The *Chronicle* seemed to ignore major events that did not affect the town directly. Russia was an important ally of Britain and France in the Great War. The tsar, Nicholas II, a cousin of George V, was forced to abdicate in mid-March following the February Revolution of 1917. The severe losses of the Imperial Army in the Great War (almost 3,500,000 men by the end of the war) and the incompetence of those in command finally turned public opinion in Russia against the tsar, who was seen as being responsible for the economic and military collapse of the country. Although he and his family were not executed until July 1918, his abdication sent shockwaves throughout Europe and altered Russia's contribution to the war. In early March, the British captured Baghdad and ten days later they captured much of Mesopotamia. However, they failed to capture the city of Gaza during the First Battle of Gaza on 29 March. The British had another go with the Second Battle of Gaza on 19 April, but Ottoman defences held. The Canadians, however, won an important victory at the Battle of Vimy Ridge in mid-April.

It was clearly obvious that, despite pleas to the contrary, selfishness and hoarding of food, as well as shortages, was occurring, and that as food stocks were alarmingly low, there had to be some sort of food control or even rationing. This was welcomed by a number of people. Sugar was very scarce and everyone was rationed to ½lb (about ¼kg) of sugar per week. Flour, tea and bread were also in short supply. The new loaf that had been introduced had not proved popular. Coal was rationed and sweets were prohibited. Gluttony, it was said, should be abhorred.

Those who were better off should buy the dearer cuts of meat and leave the cheaper cuts for those with less money. There was a great deal of condemnation of unpatriotic speculators and profiteers who bought and hoarded potatoes, beans and dry goods, to force up the prices. Andrew Bonar Law announced that Britain 'may have to suffer hardships unknown so far', and self-rationing of food was advocated. In May the king issued a proclamation, which was read out in every town and city, and asked the people 'to reduce the consumption of bread in their respective families by at least one fourth of the quantity consumed in ordinary times[...]and to abstain from the use of flour in pastry'.

It was advised that folk should limit themselves to one large slice of bread per day and to reduce the cakes, biscuits and tarts they bought or baked at home.

A national food controller had now been appointed and a set of new food regulations was laid down. Later, a local food control committee was appointed, which had to deal with adherence to the new regulations, supply, distribution and fair prices:

- output of beer limited to a third of the output in the period 1 April 1915 – 31 March 1916
- the manufacture and sale of malt was prohibited, except under licence
- barley, oats and maize were to be used only as seed, human or animal food
- imported beans, peas and lentils were taken over by the Ministry of Food
- bread was not to be sold until it had been made for twelve hours
- loaves allowed were tin, one piece, oven bottom, pan Coburg and twin sister brick
- rolls had to weigh not less than one ounce and not more than two ounces
- no currants, sultanas or sugar in bread and no milk bread allowed
- all bread to be sold by weight and all loaves must weigh 1lb or an even number of pounds
- no wheat, rye, rice, tapioca, sago or arrowroot to be used, except as human food
- fancy cakes, muffins and crumpets were prohibited
- 15 per cent sugar was allowed in cakes and biscuits, but only 10 per cent in scones
- Food Control to oversee all imported cheese
- no hoarding

- feeding stuffs for horses rationed
- maximum wholesale price of milk was to be 6½ d per gallon (65p); retail 3½ d per quart (34p)
- meat sales subject to a number of regulations
- publicly sold meals also subject to various regulations
- sugar allowed per person reduced to 25 per cent of 1915 supply
- tea and coffee to be sold by net weight

Easter arrived quite late in mid-April and brought little respite. The local paper described with gusto the 'arctic Easter weather'. Already depressed, under-fed and hard-up, few Glossop people made Easter visits to anywhere and the number of holidaymakers fell by four fifths on the previous year's total. The food controller prohibited the sale of all fancy pastries and cakes and bread was rationed to three slices a day. Food shops, except those selling eel and tripe, were forced to close early 'to avoid food wastage'. By May, public meals i.e. meals in cafes, canteens, public institutions, were rationed. Meat was limited to 5oz (140g) per person and bread to 2oz (56g). Teacakes, crumpets, muffins

Co-operative Stores (main town branch) facing Norfolk Square, Glossop, c1910.

and pastries were forbidden. Cakes and buns could only have 16 per cent sugar and scones were to have no sugar added at all. Any decoration of such foods was forbidden. Glossop folk joined the sombre mood of the rest of the country. Then it was announced that there were problems in obtaining sufficient seed potatoes for all the Glossopdale/Hadfield/Padfield allotments. Glossopians were desperately worried. Rising prices and food economies were already biting hard and there was a real fear voiced that soon people would begin to actually starve. Deprivation was already taking its toll on health. There was a severe outbreak of measles in St James and All Saints wards. At the height of the epidemic there were 480 children ill, of whom seven died. There was also an outbreak of scarlet fever, with a total of eighty-one cases. The incidence of tuberculosis rose, the clinic on Surrey Street dealing with 112 patients from May 1916 – May 1917, and several attacks of influenza were reported. Ironically, at the same time, Moorfields Military Hospital was selected for a special study of the diseases of trench fever and trench foot suffered by soldiers who had to spend considerable periods of time in the trenches at least knee-deep in water.

Troubles continued for the cotton industry, formerly Glossop's main employer. Glossop District Weavers, Winders and Warpers lost a good many of their number who went to work in munitions factories. Greenfield Mill in Hadfield was now devoted to the manufacture of munitions. So too were Waterside Mills. Those workers who switched received an extra half pence (5p) an hour in wages. The cotton winders then went on strike at Wood's Howard Town Mill, requesting more money for an increased workload. A week later, cotton and woollen workers went on strike for a 20 per cent advance on wages, which had previously been refused, and threatened to resign if they were not paid. The problem was that the whole cotton trade industry was facing the same difficulties of less employment and wages not meeting the costs of high food prices. There was also concern over a shortage in the raw cotton supply. Less was being grown in the United States due to high costs and the ravages of insects, and not enough had been done to ensure that sufficient quantities of cotton grown in Egypt, India and Sudan would make up the supply.

Like most towns Glossop had a Suffragette association, which had put most of its work on hold while its members helped in the war effort, but that had never ceased to make the point that women could do the work that the men did just as efficiently. Women were working equally as hard and equally as effectively as men in medicine, munitions,

Glossop Grammar School, c1911, where the offending German memorial plaque was placed in 1907.

teaching and the factories, and this also proved to be the case in agriculture, even though women often earned far less than men. The case of the Suffragettes was proved time and again and the male establishment began to accept that it was 'becoming imperative that they [women] should have a voice in future legislation.' By the summer of 1917, the government had at last realised what a debt of gratitude was owed to the women of England for 'keeping the home fires burning', doing many of the jobs previously done by men, and so much more besides, while the men were away fighting. In fact the chief inspector of factories and workshops in 1916 admitted 'the great adaptability of women in substitution'. Finally the proposed changes to the Electoral Reform Bill were to become law and women over the age of 30 were to get the vote. The property qualification, i.e. needing to be a property owner in order to vote, was also abolished.

The war was becoming increasingly bitter as casualties increased daily and no progress seemed to be made, although soldiers could not write home of the dangers and discomforts they faced or what they considered the real situation to be on the battlefields of France for fear of affecting public morale but it was impossible to contain all their conflicting feelings and emotions. A glimpse of what they were going through could be seen from the outburst in a letter written anonymously to the *Glossop Chronicle* in June by a soldier who had been wounded at Ypres. Before the war he had attended Glossop Grammar School. In 1907 a boy named as Will Fielding, who had been the school's first senior prefect, was killed in a climbing accident in Germany. Fielding's German companions had sent a wooden wreath with a German flag behind it attached to a plaque to the school in memory of their dead colleague, which had been placed on the wall in the Second Form classroom. The soldier's wrath boiled over as he described 'this most ugly wreath', and he expressed his outrage that a German flag had been retained behind this wreath, saying that the 'Glossop lad was disgraced by contact with such vile rubbish', and demanding its removal. Whether or not this was done temporarily is not recorded but, although it is now no longer in situ, there are several memories of its existence on the premises until well into the late twentieth century.

The Whitsun weekend of 1917 had good summer weather and Glossopians took advantage of the sunshine to try and lift their dampened spirits. The paper shortage was acute and local newspapers were reduced to four pages formed by a single piece of broadsheet folded in half. Details of both news and local activities were greatly curtailed, although room was still found for advertisements for it was these that kept the newspapers going. Rumours of a potato crop, blighted in the Peak District by a plague of caterpillars, seemed to have abated and Glossop farmers were praised for devoting their land to the cultivation of food crops and for the quality of their potato crops. Potatoes were now in good supply and could be served on any day of the week and in public eating places.

The situation regarding bread was not so cheerful. The cabbage fly had been busy causing grief with the grain crops and wheat flour was in even shorter supply. The government's decree that no more than 50 per cent of wheat flour (in some cases only 30 per cent) should be used in the making of bread, cakes and scones, had resulted in 'musty' flour as a result of being mixed with too much rice or bean flour. This caused much of the bread to be dry and tasteless and it didn't do much for the flavour of cakes or scones either.

The authorities realised that the war was going to last for at least another year and the government now required even more acreage for growing food. Lord Howard offered to pay half the cost of ploughing across his land which, in effect, meant the whole of Glossopdale. Seed potato distribution was also going well and there were good prospects for the harvest this year. Advice was given on vegetable storage. Quite a number of Glossopdale farmers and allotment-holders took to keeping bees as well, since it had been announced that honey was to be a sugar substitute for jams and preserves.

Towards the end of July it was as though the *Glossop Chronicle* and its readers had become so punch-drunk with the dreadful injuries and terrible details emerging from the battle zones, and all the deprivations at home, that they focused at length on the legal proceedings for the diversion of a footpath from High Street West to Higher Dinting, which passed by one end of the Wren Nest Mills. The details were completely parochial and never-ending, but they caused great passion. It was a reaction similar to that of deep shock. It is a well-known phenomenon that after some traumatic event, like a car crash or perhaps an explosion, people will focus on tiny irrelevant details like whether they had made the bed or done the washing up. The mood persisted into the first weeks of August when the *Chronicle* published articles on the discovery that death and injury could be caused by rushing wind from flying objects and on the peculiarities of spinning tops always pointing to the North Star, the Pole Star. However, after peace talks, which had been initiated by the pope, broke down amid claims that they had been 'a folly', both the local paper and the local people seemed to calm themselves and returned to dealing with life and 'the war to end all wars' as best they could.

After the tragedy of the Somme and the bombardment of London by heavy-duty German Gotha G IV planes, as well as the unending bitter fighting, George V was faced with a difficult and painful decision. In the wake of his cousin, Tsar Nicholas II, abdicating from the Russian throne as a result of the February Revolution that had followed upon the assassination of Rasputin at the end of December in 1916, the king was also facing the embarrassing prospect of continuing to fight another of his cousins, Kaiser Wilhelm, with whom he privately got on rather well. After the bombings and the tragedy of the Somme, anti-German feeling was running extremely high in Britain and it was felt that it was too much to ask the British people to follow and fight for a king of German descent and bearing the very German name of Saxe-Coburg-Gotha. George V couldn't help his lineage but he could make a very public gesture of renouncing his German connections. On 17 July 1917 he issued a royal proclamation:

> Now, therefore, We, out of Our Royal Will and Authority, do hereby declare and announce that as from the date of this Our Royal Proclamation, Our House and Family shall be styled and known as the House and Family of Windsor, and that all the descendants in the male line of Our said Grandmother, Queen Victoria, who are subjects of this realm[...]shall bear the said Name of Windsor.

On 31 July, the infamous Battle of Passchendaele began in Flanders. David Lloyd George opposed the battle but Field Marshall Sir Douglas Haig was in favour. The whole battle lasted as long as the Battle of the Somme had until Canadian troops finally captured Passchendaele in November. The British managed to breach the Hindenburg Line at the Battle of Cambrai on 20 November, with the first successful use of tanks. Nearly 250,000 British men and 300,000 Germans were killed, injured, maimed or listed as missing. Although the Allies won it was something of a hollow victory and David Lloyd George later wrote:

> Passchendaele was indeed one of the greatest disasters of the War[...]no soldier of any intelligence now defends this senseless campaign.

John McRae's poem In Flanders Field, written in 1915 still held true:

> In Flanders fields the poppies blow
> between the crosses, row on row,
> that mark our place[...]we are the dead...

There was a lot of labour unrest as a result of the still rising food prices, profiteering and a fear of displacement. The working classes felt that they were paying far more than their fair share for the war. This badly affected morale in places like Glossop, which was just a small northern mill town now struggling for survival. Due to the lack of housing with baths or water closets, pleas were made for more commodious public baths so that people could at least try to keep themselves reasonably clean. Food committees were set up locally for the distribution of bread, meat and sugar and also to regulate prices. The potato blight had returned with a vengeance to the High Peak, but celery and marrow crops were thriving. The killing of wild and migratory birds for food had now been authorised by the government to eke out food supplies, so the curlew, whose soulful cries so characterised the open moorlands, golden plover, woodcock and mallards were a welcome addition to the meagre food

Mark IV tank identical to that given to Glossop, 1919

supplies. The shortage of coal was causing grave concern and local households were urged to try and buy coal regularly and gradually save up stocks for the winter. As the annual Wakes holiday approached (18-25 August), a letter appeared in the Chronicle asking Glossopians to buy coal rather than spend cash on holidays. After all, the letter-writer went on to say, the troops got no holidays so why should civilians indulge themselves. The plea was unnecessary. Few had the spare cash for holidays and those who did have any money were using it to buy food and fuel anyway. Besides which, public morale was at a low ebb and many families were grieving for lost or missing members, although some folk did treat themselves with a trip to Manchester. To try and provide a little diversion and entertainment for Wakes week, Moorfields and Partington hospitals decided to challenge each other to a Wakes cricket match in aid of their own funds and tea would be provided. The team from each hospital was to consist of ten soldiers and five nurses. The match was keenly anticipated and well-attended. Moorfields won with ninety-two runs against Partington's more modest forty runs.

Elsewhere the news was a bit more depressing. Glossop Football Club was sold for £450 (£11,075), a tiny amount compared with the multimillion pound deals of today. It was a shame. Other football clubs and teams in the area remained well-supported, most notably Stalybridge Celtic just 5 miles away, which is still a thriving club today. The annual ceremony of Whitfield well-dressing was discontinued, due to both lack of enthusiasm and concerns expressed for the harvest. Glossop was always susceptible to rainfall, more so than many other places, because it lay on a boundary where the flatter agricultural lands of the Cheshire Plain met the high hills of the Dark Peak. There had been heavy summer rainfall this year and a bad harvest was feared. However, while the corn crops were affected the root crops had thrived and the townsfolk managed to grow a very large crop of peas. Some local farmers decided to expand their stock of sheep to try and compensate, because they could graze the sheep up on the Glossop and Woodhead moorlands where the soil (such as there was) was unsuitable for crop-growing. The Chronicle lamented the ever growing lists of casualties in 'this terrible armageddon', and the news from the Front seemed to get graver by the week. The cotton industry was also in trouble. In Glossop mills, 40 per cent of the looms were stopped and the staff worked in rotation. This caused grave concerns over reduced pay and it was agreed that grants of between 19/- (£23.38) and 25/- (£30.76) should be paid to affected workers. These grants were considered too low against the high food and fuel prices. Milk was 6.d (67p) for just under a litre and bread was 4.5 d (46p) for a loaf weighing a little under a kilo. For a family of four people, bread and milk for the week might cost between a quarter and a third of their wages grant, the equivalent of someone bringing home £300 a week in wages today spending nearly £100 per week on two basic food essentials. Cheddar, Cheshire and Lancashire cheese sold at 1s 7d (£1.95) a pound (half a kg) and beef dripping at 1s 4d (£1.64) a pound (½kg). Coal cost 8s6d (£12.87) per ton. Coffee, at 2s 6d (£3.08) per pound (½kg) made it little more than a luxury for most. Butter cost the same. The colour of the war brand of flour was described as 'objectionable' and the local Co-operative Wholesale Society threatened to produce their own brand of white flour against government regulations. Although this would cost more, at least folk would be able to eat some decent bread again.

Local authority cuts in spending were biting hard. Little maintenance work on housing stock or water closet conversions had been carried out in Glossop since the war began, and the disposal of sewage was mostly still done by night waste carts, which posed a high risk of disease. There were numerous accidents in the darkened streets. On moonless nights it was almost impossible to see where one was going. A bylaw was passed saying that pedestrians should pass each other on the right. Those on the left could feel their way along the walls of buildings but those on the right had no means of guidance and frequently fell off the pavements, often into the path of traffic. It is difficult to imagine this today because of the amount of street lighting in use, but those who have been to remote British islands where there are no street lights will understand how dark the night can be, especially when cloud cover hides even the starlight. Then in late November a reader of the *Glossop Chronicle*, who signed himself 'Descipulus Marcus', complained that the local library did not stock the Greek or Roman Classical writers and he began a campaign for a 'readable library'. Few seemed to agree with his sentiments. The library was, in any case, now only open for three hours a day (Monday – Friday 5 – 8pm), which did not seem to maximise the hours of daylight, and from 2 – 5pm on Saturdays. Ironically, at the same time, an appeal for books and magazines for the troops was begun. The paper shortage meant that current newspapers and magazines were severely curtailed, some even ceasing publication, and so past numbers were eagerly sought after.

The late summer and autumn had seen fierce fighting with the Third Battle of Ypres, the First, Second and Third Battles of Passchendaele, the Battle of Cambrai and the Third Battle of Gaza. The latter had begun with the Battle of Beersheba on Halloween and the Third Battle of Gaza eventually ended on 7 November, when the British finally broke through the Ottoman lines. While all this was going on, Russia was having very serious problems. Industrial production was down a third on the previous year. As many as 50 per cent of industrial centres were closed, especially in the Urals. There were strikes by miners, metal workers, oil workers, textile workers and railroad workers. The country was on the verge of bankruptcy and had suffered enormous manpower losses in the war. Since the tsar had abdicated in February, a provisional government had been based in his former home, the Winter Palace in Petrograd. At the end of October the Bolsheviks finally seized power, storming the Winter Palace in a symbolic gesture. Afterwards the tsar and his family were imprisoned at Yekaterinburg until their executions in 1918. All of this seemed to be a long way from Glossop and barely merited mention on the local papers but, as ever, Glossopian thoughts were centred much nearer to home.

There had been 'a fine letter about our heroes in Mesopotamia' published in the *Glossop Chronicle* a despatch about the fall of

Messines, and a moving account of a Hadfield soldier's experiences on the Holy Land in addition to a letter published on the front page about 'Glossop Heroes to Palestine'. The war work of all Derbyshire women, particularly those in Glossopdale, was praised for both their efforts on the manufacture of munitions and the number of 'valuable comforts' that they sewed and knitted for the troops (nightshirts, underwear, socks, mufflers, etc). Isaac Jackson of Hawkshead Mill in the older part of Glossop paid to replace a horse-drawn ambulance with a motor ambulance named the Isaac Jackson Ambulance and this was seen as an act of great generosity.

Now, as yet another Christmas at war approached, fundraising began in earnest to try and send some Christmas treats to the troops serving abroad. Glossopians gave generously, as they always did, for the Christmas boxes. But at the same time everyone was asked to save 6d (about 62p) every week for the war loan. The town had a population of around 21,700 at this time and had been issued with a quota of national war bonds worth £10,800 (£265,800). The town's purchase of these bonds had fallen well below the target and the council was instructed to take action. The chief concerns of most hard-pressed families in Glossopdale were with feeding themselves, trying to keep warm and ensuring their 'lads overseas' were not neglected. They had been less than impressed with rumours of economic inefficiencies at national level while at local level so many were struggling. The Glossop allotments project was going well and producing more food than expected, so they were astonished to be told of the local council's plea to contribute more to the war effort, of a national plea to grow even more food and to receive an order to 'dig deep, dig more and dig harder'. Saving money for war bonds as well was perhaps a step too far for most Glossopdale citizens.

It was a quiet and subdued Christmas for the town that year. Most people were short of money and some were short of food. Many were dispirited that there still seemed to be no end in sight to the war, and those who had managed to save something for a small treat or outing at Christmas time were dismayed to be told that not only would the number of rail journeys be considerably reduced for reasons of economy and fuel conservation, but that preference would be given to soldiers travelling to and from leave. It was forbidden to use petrol for pleasure or for non-essential journeys and the police had powers to stop cars and to confiscate the vehicle if it was being driven for frivolous purposes. The message was clear. Stay at home. The only concession for the festive

**Great War Memorial
Hadfield, near Glossop,
erected c1922.**

season was that the local police allowed a few streetlamps to be lit, probably in response to the number of accidents occurring to pedestrians. The mayoress, Mrs Partington, now in her third term of office, managed to ensure that food and Christmas parcels were despatched to the troops in time for most of them to reach their destination before Christmas Day. News had filtered through that in many places supplies were a shambles and little allowance was made to try and give the fighting men something extra. At home there was the distinct feeling that not only had this war become a terrible financial burden, but it was the poorest in the country who were helping to fund it the most. While there was no resentment of anything that helped the troops, there was considerable unrest about the constant reports that the government was squandering money through inefficient management.

There were also serious concerns voiced by many over gross inequalities in food distribution at home and it beginning to be considered that compulsory food rationing was necessary. Then it was announced that in the New Year food cards would be distributed on which weekly supplies of sugar, tea, butter, bacon, flour, jam, syrup, tinned milk and matches would be marked for each person. Folk would deposit these with a designated shopkeeper of their choice and then collect their rations on a weekly basis.

Despairing questions were asked as the war dragged on. It was felt that the country had lost its way and that there was far too much profiteering going on. Morale was suffering because of all the sacrifices and yet there seemed to be no end in sight.

Chapter Five

1918

THE FIRST WEEK of January was the first week for years that the *Glossop Chronicle* had not reported any war casualties. Either no news had reached them or they just wanted to try and lift spirits a little by sparing their readers the tragic and depressing gloom of the seemingly never-ending war for just a few days more. There were, however, a number of letters from soldiers thanking the townsfolk warmly for their Christmas gifts and voicing appreciation that the folks back home cared so much. The censors were very strict and the letters never described the conditions in which the troops were living and fighting, nor the type of gifts that they had received. In fact many of the letters were anonymous, although it is certain that almost everyone would have signed their name. Still, it was a link, however tenuous, with those who could not share Christmas with their loved ones.

Back home the Glossop butchers went on strike for two days in protest at what they considered to be unrealistically low wholesale meat prices. Eventually the local food control committee agreed to amendments so that the butchers would have a small profit margin. This, of course, would have to be paid for through higher retail prices, which would be yet another blow for already hard-pressed housewives. To add to the restrictions, the sale of cream was forbidden by the Glossop food control committee unless it was for children under 5, invalids or for making butter. And to lessen the demand for traditionally made butter, the food control committee suggested the use of potato butter, which cost about 5d (about 42p) for a pound (just under ½kg). Potato butter was made by sieving and mashing a number of large potatoes and adding a teaspoon of salt and 2oz (about 60g) of real butter or margarine. The result was a letter to the *Glossop Chronicle* saying that a municipal distribution centre, open to both shoppers and tradesmen, should replace the expensive officials who were forever snooping on prices. This received the equally tart reply that since there were no grumbles from the sailors being killed or injured to try and keep the country supplied with foodstuffs then the grumblers at home should simply shut up.

The question of food supplies had now become paramount. In 1917 the Germans bombarded British merchant shipping with the use of submarine warfare and had sunk thousands of tons of shipping laden with food and other supplies. People trespassed on local allotments and stole food despite a prohibitive fine of £100 (£2,020).The government tried a system of voluntary rationing, in which the Royal family themselves took part and even suggested some of the standards. It didn't work and there were problems with price rigging and the improper sharing of scarce or restricted goods. In January sugar was rationed, for which cards were issued, while tea, flour and butter were in short supply. There were claims of 'selfishness and avarice on the part of those who took more than their fair share' by shopping in several places and offering financial inducements. The result, of course, was that richer members of the population did well while malnutrition started to show among the poorer members. The government took further action and in February Glossop schools acted as distribution centres for tea and butter cards to be issued upon production of sugar ration cards but this time with the proviso that the ration cards must be left with the person's shopkeeper of choice. The local Co-operative Society undertook to ensure 'equitable distributions of sugar, tea, butter, margarine, flour'. Housewives were now expected to include at least 10 per cent of potato flour in all their baking. Only one ounce of tea (about 30g or the modern equivalent of around ten tea bags) was allowed per person per week. The Co-operative Society was short of butter, bacon, boots and coal due to the large amount of supplies commandeered for the war effort. In London a box of twenty-nine strawberries cost £2 10s (£50.48) and in Glossop a pound (just under ½kg) of tobacco cost £7 10s (£151.43).

The Ministry of Food, under the leadership of Lord Rhondda, a survivor of the Lusitania, as minister of food control, finally decided that food rationing really was unavoidable and issued forms to be filled in by every household in the land. Every customer had to register with one shop to purchase certain foodstuffs and, once registered, could not go elsewhere for them. No shopkeeper was required to register more customers than they could properly handle. Supplies would be distributed to the shopkeepers in proportion to the number of customers they had and each shopkeeper was required to divide all weekly supplies proportionately among those registered. Initially margarine, butter, bacon and meat would be rationed in addition to sugar, which had been rationed for some time, but there were delays in issuing the food coupons and organising equitable distribution. The Co-operative Society had already been complaining of unfair food distributions. In mid-February, Lord Rhondda ordered a voluntary surrender of hoarded food, but this met with only muted success. A milk priority scheme was initiated and, in accordance with Lord Rhondda's directives, local bakers met to decide how they could utilise their existing machinery to use potato flour for making bread, using perhaps just a fraction of wheat flour. Lord Rhondda also designated Wednesdays and Fridays as 'meatless days for the provinces', when no meat could be served in public eating establishments. Rationing finally became official on 21 March and, after much complicated form-filling, everyone received ration books, without which they could not obtain any of the rationed foodstuffs.

Extra allotments in Glossop were given as part of the 3,000 extra acres in the Peak District that were to be ploughed for food production, and those who worked them were told to 'grow vegetables for victory'. There was a problem, however. The summer of 1917 had been dry and local springs had not been replenished by rainwater. Lord Howard said that although the water supply for Ludworth would be increased by providing an extra bore-hole, folks were not to water their allotments. Hens were barred from Glossop allotments and there were requests to grow more onions. There was also a celery leaf blight, which didn't help matters. Neither did the vandalism suffered at Dinting Allotments but local farmers, allotment owners and the Land Army girls sowed extra potato and vegetable crops and hoped for the best. Glossop District Farmers had 167 members and all of them were concerned that milk was selling at 1/- (£1.01) a gallon (just under 4l) while production costs were 1s 8d (about £1.68). Milk was also more expensive for the public to buy in Glossop than in Manchester by 1d (8 or 9p) per quart (just under a litre). They said that a cattle market was desperately needed in Glossop. The food control committee agreed and recommended that Lord Howard open Glossop market on Tuesdays and Saturdays as a cattle market and a grading station. The farmers also requested a drying kiln and rolling mills to be set up in the district in order to extract as much food as possible from locally grown crops.

The cotton trade was, in its own words, just 'hanging on'. Glossop weavers questioned if the cloth carriers were paid enough and believed that they should earn 7d or 8d (around 56p or 65p) per four-loom weaver. The cloth carriers themselves were holding out for 6d (about 48p) per four-loom weaver. The mill owners were reluctant to pay anything like that and insisted that 1.5d (12p) was their top offer. In the end the weavers decided to dispense with the services of the carriers and do the carrying work themselves as a protest, but it removed yet another source of earning potential which, while the rewards were very small, was at least better than nothing. It also slowed down the production of individual weavers as they now had to spend time fetching and carrying their own cloth. Glossop weavers put up a fierce resistance to the minimum age for working in the mills to be lowered from 15 to 14. It was, after all, barely fifty years since children had been freed from working in the mills and the older cotton workers simply saw it as a way of getting cheaper labour. Mills using American cotton supplies were told to reduce output by a further 10 per cent which meant that they were now working at just 50 per cent capacity. It was not a good time for anyone to be asking for wage rises but members of Glossop town council chose this moment to request salary increases. To most people's disbelief this was granted and Glossop rates subsequently went up by 4d (32p) in the pound (240 old pence in 1918).

Towards the end of February the British captured Jericho. In the first week of February the *Glossop Chronicle* published a letter full of detail, which had somehow managed to get past the censors, from a Gamesley corporal serving with the Mesopotamian Expeditionary Force. Mesopotamia was the name given to the area between the Tigris and Euphrates Rivers, which today covers modern Iraq, a little of Iran (formerly Persia), north-east Syria and part of south-east Turkey. The corporal was anxious to describe the life of his Eastern counterparts and wrote:

> The Indians are clean and fastidious and civilised[...]Arabs are virile, vigorous, independent and won't be pushed around[..].' But he went on, '[...]life is primitive and often nomadic, industry is primitive, villages, for the most part, are mere dumps for refuse[...]there is no idea of sanitary arrangements.

Nomadic tribes tend to bury their sewage waste in the earth and this last observation was somewhat ironic coming from a man whose home was in an area where the use of pails for toilets was prevalent and the pails were then tipped into barrels to be tipped into a pit in the earth and covered.

A few weeks later there was another letter to the *Chronicle* from a local soldier serving abroad saying that the Russian soldiers were, in fact, much cleaner than their British, Belgian and French counterparts, because the Russian authorities provided 'bath trains' for their troops. These trains 'had four bath cars and cars for washing and disinfecting laundry', plus hot water besides.

A curious little item appeared in the *Chronicle* published on 22 February 1918. There was a letter from Commander John Ireland to

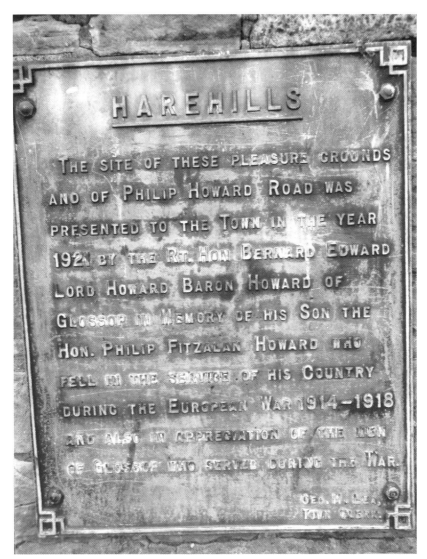

Harehills Park, the gift of Lord Howard to Glossop, c1922, in memory of his son, Philip Howard, and the soldiers of Glossop who died in the Great War.

Commander D. Coy in Glossop thanking him for services rendered 'when planes landed at Padfield (near Glossop) on Tuesday last', and the chief constable, John C. Hodgson, confirmed that police 'had guarded the aeroplanes until they left'. No details of the planes were given, their numbers, their nationality or what they were doing. There was no other mention anywhere else of such an incident taking place nor were there any photographs. There were still Zeppelin raids taking place over Lancashire as late as 1918 and it is possible that the planes might have been a part of a secret mission against the Germans. Whatever the truth this strange little incident was never explained. Perhaps the biggest clue might lie in the fact that the letter was addressed to the Commander of D. Coy instead of D. Company.

On 3 March, Leon Trotsky signed a peace treaty with Germany. The Russians had problems of their own at home and were still undecided what to do about the deposed tsar. The tsar had asked George V for asylum in England for himself and his family, but, although on a personal level, as the tsar's cousin, the king had wanted to agree, he knew that it would be political suicide to do so and so, reluctantly, he had declined the request. Eventually, on 17 July, the tsar and his family were executed by the Bolsheviks. On 1 April, the Royal Flying Corps and the Royal Naval Air Service combined to form the Royal Air Force. It was becoming clear the Allies were in the ascendant but neither the German forces nor those of the Austro-Hungarians or the Ottomans were prepared to go quietly. There were further battles fought on the Marne and the Somme in France and against the Turks at Baku.

The women of Glossopdale, along with the rest of the Derbyshire women, despite their hardships and privations made the most amazing efforts to help keep the troops supplied with warm and comfortable clothing. Each month the Derbyshire county clearing house had been distributing 7 miles (around 12km) of flannel, 1 ton of knitting wool (apx 1,016kg) and 3 cwt (about 153kg) of knitting cotton from which, by April 1918, the women had produced over 1,000,000 garments and comforters for the soldiers and sailors fighting in the war. It was perhaps appropriate that the women's achievements were acknowledged in the same month that women were admitted to the parliamentary franchise on the new electoral role for the first time. It was an incredible achievement and acknowledged as such. What many thought, but no one said, at least publicly, was that it had all been done voluntarily out of love, duty and patriotism. Women had been working equally as hard and effectively as men in medicine, munitions, teaching, the factories and agriculture, even though they often earned far less than men. The case of the Suffragettes was proved time and again and the male establishment had finally accepted it was 'imperative that they should have a voice in future legislation'. Women could at last legally vote for their country. Although a few classes of both men and women were not finally enfranchised until 1928, no one was any longer disqualified from voting for receiving poor law relief or alms (basic welfare benefits). In Glossop the electorate more than doubled its numbers, from around 4,000 to over 10,000 voters. Excited first-time voters would have to wait, however, for no municipal elections were to be held in 1918. As the icing on the cake, in the same month the girls and women of the Land Army were also praised for the amount of food they had produced from the land. An unexpected but nevertheless welcome side effect of the Land Army was that it abolished class differences between members. Debutantes and factory girls worked alongside each other as equals and welcomed the friendships that grew as a result.

Production of food continued to remain a major issue. By the end of April, rationing of cheese had been added to that of butter, margarine, meat, tea, sugar and flour. The Glossop food control committee applied for higher rations of butter and margarine because large numbers of the townspeople had to eat their meal (sandwiches) in the mills and factories, although it was possible, by using homemade chutneys and pickles, to disguise the lack of butter or margarine in butties, as Glossop folk termed their sandwiches. There was some discussion of the possibility of using cocoa butter in cooking as a substitute for proper butter, but it was discounted due to the fact that cocoa butter smells very strongly of cocoa.

There was now an annual ration of 200 eggs per person (less than four eggs per week) and this had to include eggs used in cooking. A club was formed in Glossop to breed rabbits for extra food. Mainly, however, housewives and cooks relied on the supply of fresh fruit and vegetables. Tasty soup could be made from carrots, onions, rice, pepper, mace, 1oz (about 30g) of bacon and a good stock made from boiling meat bones. A filling savoury pudding was made from beans, stale bread, potatoes, onions, carrots, fresh parsley, pepper and a little bacon or sausage meat. Stewed fruit, rice pudding or a potato pudding made from flour, mashed potato, suet, treacle and milk, were served as desserts. Although the daily diet was meagre and a number of people lost some weight, an unexpected bonus of rationing was that malnutrition among the poorer classes and the scourge of rickets disappeared because everyone was entitled to at least some of the important and essential foodstuffs, even if only a small share. Ironically, a century after the Great War, malnutrition and rickets have become issues once again, although this time due to changes in eating habits and a lack of culinary skills rather than lack of supplies or poverty.

The Whitsun holidays of 1918 in Glossop were mostly spent at home due to food rationing, travel restrictions and the fact that most people had very little spare cash. As it happened it was fortuitous for there was heavy rainfall and hailstorms damaged newly planted allotment seedlings. Bridgefield Allotments in Glossop suffered particularly badly. Boys of secondary school age were now helping to work on the local allotments so that their peers could respond to the latest call-up requirements. The rabbits for food project was proving successful and helping to eke out the meat supplies. There was active promotion for keeping rabbits and good rabbit food could be found in the waste produce of the allotment workings. Some frozen meat was now being sold with strict warnings that it must be de-frosted thoroughly before cooking and that slow cooking was absolutely essential. As the summer progressed, the potato crop flourished in Glossopdale but dwarf kidney beans did badly. Generally, though, food production from local allotments was good. Agriculture was no longer the Cinderella of the home industries and it was proving that, with hard work and restraint, the country could become self-sufficient. Even the quality of the bread was improved and loaves were reduced from 2s 6d (£2.50) to 2s 4d (around £2.33).

A sinister development in July 1918 was the first mention in Glossop of the Spanish influenza outbreak, which peaked in 1919 killing millions around the world. It was believed that a little coffee burned on hot coals would purify a sick room and this is what was advised where possible. Local schools closed due to outbreaks of influenza, whooping cough and mumps. In the crowded living conditions of many people, outbreaks spread quickly as there was no room to isolate a sick person and, although doctors were aware of the benefits, most folk did not really understand the importance of isolation. Veno's was promoted as a cure for the Spanish flu but, in reality, like more modern preparations, it only alleviated the symptoms for a time rather than cured them. Then, as now, defeat of the flu virus was down to the immune system of individuals. While the rationing of foodstuffs had improved the quality of nutrition, the quantities allowed, and the lower intake of first class proteins from meat and dairy products, had weakened resistance to germs in many folk and they succumbed more readily to illness.

The war news and lists of casualties continued to be grim. A number of families had now lost more than one member, and some had lost several. Warfare in the skies was a phenomena that first occurred during the Great War and a local man, Charles Barlow, was hailed for having flown on three raids to destroy Zeppelins and the sheds that housed them. A brief moment of humour was caused by a Glossop lad serving in France who wrote home that he had finally realised 'the French, though foreign, are human too!' All men over military age were called to assist with the harvest. Nutshells and fruit stones were collected and used for conversion to the charcoal used for anti-gas masks. Lloyd George told the general population to 'hold fast' and that 'victory prospects were bright', but still the 'painful sensations' caused by war casualties continued.

Nationally the coal shortage had become more acute and serious than the food shortage. Gas, coal, coke and electricity were all rationed and therefore fuel and light requisition forms had to be issued, completed and handed in to the long-suffering Post Office. The heavy drain of men for call-up had crippled the mining industry in England. Taking 75,000 men from the pits had resulted in a drop of 20,000,000 tons in output every year. While the needs of the army might outweigh individual needs, industry and munitions factories had also been badly affected. It was stressed that economies in the use of coal, coke, gas and electricity were absolutely vital. Reserve stocks had been partly used and now the country could not fulfil its quota due to be sent to the Allies in Europe. A coal rationing committee and overseer were appointed in Glossop and there were plans for strict economies in the use of electric lighting and gas. Pleas from Glossopdale Rural District Council were made to Lord Howard for local people to be allowed to cut peat for extra fuel from his lands. Coal now cost 2s 6d (£2.50) per ton with an extra 10 pence (83p) for bagging.

Sometimes it seemed that everything in life was rationed, although in early-August there was a general relaxation in poultry rationing. Those who had fewer than fifty hens were no longer required to keep records of consumption and one bird per week for every four people in the household was allowed. This was almost a comparative luxury for Glosspdale folk. Only one ration coupon was now required whereas previously the number of coupons had depended upon the weight of the bird. Rabbits cost two coupons, venison one coupon per pound (just under ½kg), geese and turkeys three coupons per bird, ducks one coupon per bird. For other birds the coupons required depended upon the size of the bird and ranged from a brace of pheasants to sixteen snipe. Wood pigeons and rooks were not rationed. In late July there had been a glut of herrings, so fifteen barrels were distributed among the Red Cross hospitals in the Manchester area. Good news on the food front was much needed for local allotments had suffered badly from parsnip canker

War Memorial, Norfolk Square, Glossop, c1922.

blight and also from plagues of daddy longlegs, which caused considerable damage to crops.

Remembrance services were held during early-August in local churches to mark the fourth anniversary of the outbreak of war. Later in August, despite a shortage of money, Glossopians determined to try and enjoy the summer Wakes holiday in late August, although the September Wakes in the original village area, now known as Old Glossop, were cancelled. There were record bookings for trips to Manchester, which were day trips and did not involve overnight accommodation costs. A new football club was established for Glossop and Hadfield District. Wakes cricket matches were played and there seemed to be an air of cautious optimism that perhaps the Great War might soon be over. The Hundred Days Offensive began in early-August and this proved to be the last phase of the war. During the Battle of the Hindenburg Line, Allied troops had finally broken through German defences. It was the beginning of the end. Nevertheless, the Christmas gift appeals for the troops began, although there were secret hopes that some of the men might actually be

home for Christmas this year. There was an enjoyable grand fête held in Glossop Park in aid of prisoners-of-war and British Red Cross funds. Glossop also took pride in being top of the league for gold and silver collections for the Red Cross.

The Glossop, Hadfield & District Horticultural Association held a successful show in September and the allotments were praised as a credit to the town, in spite of their earlier problems with blights and insect pests. Glossop, Hadfield and District Allotment Association followed this with their second annual show at the Town Hall. Subsequently, the produce was displayed at the Victoria Hall for the week of the fête and for a week afterwards. One sour note of reality came from a correspondent to the *Glossop Chronicle*, who signed himself or herself as 'Economy', saying that no milk should be fed to cats and that, in any case, the number of cats should be reduced, but no one took much notice. In recognition of all the successful hard work by townsfolk and local farmers in growing their own, Mr and Mrs Isaac Jackson donated funds to Glossop town council to enable them to purchase the town hall, the market and the market rights, as a memorial to local troops who had so loyally and valiantly served their country.

Life at home, however, seemed to go on pretty much as usual. Pupils of Glossop Grammar School spent the autumn term growing potatoes on a patch of ground near the military hospital of Moorfields. The teachers regarded it as good horticultural training and an important contribution to the war effort. Victory might be in sight, but food shortages were far from over. The Glossop harvest festival was held later than its traditional date, but it was a fruitful harvest thanksgiving. Local allotments were doing well although there was still a problem with thefts and vandalism, which was distressing. This was in good part attributed to the absence of fathers and the greater lenience of mothers in disciplining their children. The same reason is still being given a century on to excuse the misdemeanours of youth. The value of agricultural work had been recognised through several wage rises and minimum wages fixed for female workers of 2½ to 3 pence at 14 (25p) to 6 pence at 18 (50p) per hour, but even a minimum weekly income of 36/- (£36.34) for experienced male workers did not go far. There was continuing trouble in the cotton industry. Glossop and District cotton trade were 'playing off the system' with demands for higher wages, although there were still stoppage problems and short-working. Coal prices rose again and there was much protest. Derbyshire miners threatened to close all their coal pits if a dispute at the Mill Close lead mine was not resolved. There was no relaxation of the strict street lighting regulations despite a number of accidents. A Glossop railway porter was in court for receiving 9d (about 75p) in excess rail fares but failing to pay them in to his employers. He was fined £1 (just over £20). The Glossop and Hadfield property market was severely depressed. Three two up, two down houses on Kiln Lane in Hadfield sold for a total of £400 (£8,076) for all three properties. Christmas gift fund and public memorials appeals continued to be made. Crowden School pupils held a concert to raise money for the Woodhead Soldiers Fund and St James School in Whitfield held a fundraising dance. The influenza epidemic was tightening its grip on the whole of the Peak District and Glossop did not escape. There were a number of tragic cases but the *Glossop Chronicle* made the decision not to report on the epidemic. Perhaps they thought that the townspeople had enough problems.

Something had changed, however. There seemed to be a growing optimism and a conviction that the end of the war was finally in sight and the good fighting spirit of the British was remarked upon in several quarters.

Encouraged by this news, perhaps, the government announced that parliamentary elections would take place in October, although this was later postponed until 14 December, mainly because differences in party politics had been put aside for the duration of the war and folk did not see the necessity for being sidetracked from focusing on the war by political issues. In any case, there were large numbers of voters absent serving abroad. Electoral registration forms had arrived in each household for completion and return. Maternity and Child Welfare Acts were passed that enabled grants to be made available for lying-in homes, home helps, food for mothers and infants, hospital treatment for infants and homes for children of widowed mothers, etc. This, the government believed, would attract support from the female vote. Thus emboldened, and realising that a new generation of skilled and educated youngsters would be needed to replace those who had died on the battlefield, the government also passed a new Education Bill. The employment of children under the age of 12 was now forbidden and the compulsory school leaving age was raised to 14. School fees for ordinary primary and secondary schools were abolished and provision was made for nursery schools, playing fields, game centres, school baths, school camps, medical inspections and physical and social training. It was revolutionary and met with howls of protest from the cotton trade who employed youngsters because their wages were cheap and, as they were smaller than adults, they could clean under and around machinery without it having to be stopped. The government held firm, however. The war had changed everything and now a brave new world had to be faced.

Some men in the 35-45 age group were offered special privileges if they would undertake work on the canals, but the new Military Services Act was causing real hardship to traders by calling-up men aged 41-51. It caused severe staff shortages and, in the case of one-man businesses, it was a serious problem. Folk tried to protect one-man businesses as best they could if the owner was away, but there were limits. All men aged 41-46 had to have fitness medicals and there was also a call for 15,000 men to transfer from the Volunteer Corps to the Home Services. New ration cards were due in November so new application forms for those had to be completed, especially as lard and tea were now to be rationed. Glossop, like everywhere else, groaned collectively. Folk seemed to spend half their lives filling in forms to apply for things. To add insult to injury gas prices rose as well. Industry received a 50 per cent discount and it was basically an exercise to regulate domestic usage. As always, folk thought, the ordinary consumer was paying the price.

Peace notes had been exchanged between the United States and Germany since October, but there had been some who had questioned the gesture. Are we ready for peace? they asked. There was a diversity of views on a peace settlement and the 'enormity of the post War social reconstruction work'. David Lloyd George had not been too far wide of the mark when he said that the Great War had been fought on grounds of business as much as anything else. However, on one issue everyone seemed to be united. The kaiser had to go. In August the Hundred Days Offensive had begun with the Battle of Amiens. For a month from 18 September until 17 October, the Battle of the Hindenburg Line raged and at last the Allies managed to break through the German lines. On the Eastern front, after the long drawn out Battle of Sharon, the British entered Damascus and captured the city. At the end of September Bulgaria signed an armistice with the Allies. The German alliances were beginning to crumble and three weeks later they suspended their submarine warfare. On 29 October, the Croatians, Serbians and Slovenians proclaimed their own state and the next day the Ottoman Empire signed the Armistice of Mudros. At the beginning of November both Austria and Bulgaria withdrew from the war and sued for peace

Peace Day on the Hohenzollern Bridge in Cologne, 28 June 1919.

terms with the American President Wilson. On 4 November, Austria-Hungary made peace with Italy and the Allies advanced to the Meuse. On 9 November, Kaiser Wilhelm abdicated and Germany became a republic and the following day in Austria-Hungary, Kaiser Charles 1st abdicated. The bloodiest conflict in history was all over. On 11 November, Germany signed the Armistice of Compiegne and on 12

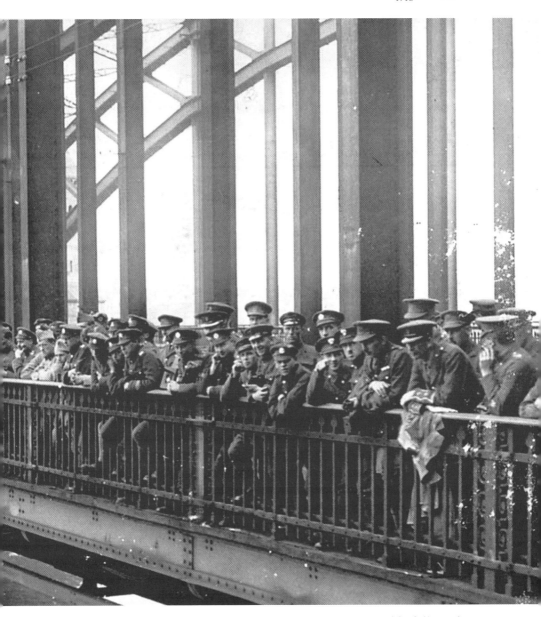

November, Austria was proclaimed a republic. Czechoslovakia followed suit two days later.

In early October the *Glossop Chronicle*, probably taking advantage of the initiative to import African and Australian grasses as new and cheaper paper-making materials, decided to treat its readers and had begun to publish an extra weekly 'pictorial supplement', which took the form of a single broadsheet folded in two filled with photographs of the war and the war efforts. The gleeful headline for the first page of the first supplement was 'Captured Huns and Guns'. Readers were told that the war had 'reached a climax' with the defeat of the Turks in Palestine. Inside there were also images of British troops with nurses in France, and photographs of the catastrophic damage inflicted by the war on France and Belgium. An amusing postscript came the following week with a story headlined 'Huns in Nuns' Clothing' about two inept German spies who had disguised themselves as nuns to try and infiltrate British Intelligence services but who had succeeded only in getting themselves arrested, thanks to the courage of a Cheshire lady. Local newspapers were still full of war news and ever-growing lists of war casualties. But now victory was openly talked about in realistic terms. However, the end of the month brought the sad news that Private Ernest Bradbury, who was serving with the Tanks Corps and who had won the Military Medal for his actions, had been reported killed in the hostilities. He was to be the last Glossopian killed in battle during the Great War.

The newly enfranchised female voters were told that politics were in 'a depraved state' but that they should support David Lloyd George to get 'a real peace'. Finally, the Germans realised they had lost. Then came the announcement for which everyone had been waiting with the immortal words of David Lloyd George, who spoke to the nation, 'at the eleventh minute of the eleventh hour of the eleventh month', to tell everyone that: 'This morning came to end the cruellest and most terrible War that has ever scourged mankind. I hope we may say that thus, this fateful morning, came an end to all wars'.

Hostilities ceased and the Great War came to an end. A hundred years later the Great War is still remembered with amazement, anguish and horror at what happened, although there is no longer any living memory of it. It brought the Edwardian era to an abrupt end and shattered a whole way of life. Amid the mud and the trenches, the appalling death toll and the crushed poppies of the battlefields lay the innocence of a civilisation, for after the Great War nothing was ever to be quite the same again. A whole generation of young men had been lost. War from the skies and chemical warfare had also been unleashed on an unsuspecting world and many old soldiers felt that 'clean honest fighting face to face' was a thing of the past. Glossop struggled to come to terms with this new world, and so did the rest of the country and the Continent. But integrity in battle had been buried somewhere out there on the battlefields with all the other bodies crushed and maimed beyond recognition.

Epilogue

1919

OVER 320 MEN from Glossop were killed in the Great War and scores more were wounded and gassed. Some recovered from their injuries, others were not so lucky. Most never talked of the horrors they witnessed or the dreadful experiences they suffered. There was no help for post-traumatic stress and no counselling services. Many, like Joseph Cooper of Glossop, who served with the Royal Welsh Fusiliers, simply tried to be stoical about the whole thing. He joined up with one of his best friends, Colin Barton, who came from nearby Marple. Colin was sent to the Gaza Strip where he was killed by a Turkish sniper's bullet late in 1917. Joseph fought in the Dardanelles. He was severely wounded and had to have a metal plate inserted in his skull, but he was one of the lucky ones. On his return to England he found that his wife, Rose, had died in the influenza pandemic. He and Colin's widow grieved together and two years later they married. They ran a grocer's shop after their marriage and had one daughter and one son. Their daughter became a Land Army Girl in World War Two. Their son served in the Merchant Navy and became a well-known science fiction writer. Joseph lived until he was 88 years old and died peacefully in his bed. There was no such happy ending for the millions of soldiers who died in the most appalling circumstances in Belgium, France and the Near East. So many corners of far and distant lands were to provide a final resting place for most, but there were many, far too many, whose bodies were never found.

After the peace and the Treaty of Versailles had been signed on Peace Day, 28 June 1919, it was decided that 265 tanks should be donated to certain towns and cities in recognition of their efforts to buy war bonds and war savings certificates. Tanks were first used at the Battle of the Somme in 1916 during the battle of Troves Wood on 15 September. They were cumbersome and liable to break down, but army engineers persevered in trying to understand how they worked and the best ways of using them. It was generally agreed that the first time tanks were used properly was at the Battle of Cambrai in November 1917. Glossop was chosen to receive a type 1917 Mk IV 'Female' tank. 'Female' tanks carried a number of machine-guns instead of the heavier armaments carried by the 'male' tanks. The tank was brought by rail from the tank depot at Bovington Camp and delivered by a crew from the Tank Corps. It was supplied without its guns and with final drive chains so it could not be used aggressively, and was placed in Glossop Park. Like all the other places that received a tank, Glossop didn't want it. The tanks were unpopular because people just wanted to forget the war, not have a permanent reminder of it and all its attendant horror in their back yard. Two hundred and sixty-four of the tanks donated lasted less than twenty years and were scrapped before the start of World War Two. The remaining one, at Ashford in Kent, survived only because it became part of an electricity sub-station.

On 19 July 1919, as it was named as the official peace day, Glossop was in festive mood and flags, bunting and banners fluttered everywhere in the town. Norfolk Square was 'very pretty', with 'archways and mottoes' at the entrance from High Street West and at the opposite entrance from Henry Street and there was 'a plenitude of colour woven into the scheme of adornment'. Shops and businesses closed and the day was declared a public holiday. The official programme included a presentation of colours by Lord Howard to the local scouts and guides, the United Choir Festival and concerts by Glossop Old Band and the Public Reed Band. The mayor planted a tree in Glossop Park to commemorate the signing of the peace treaty. The day ended at 11pm with a special display of Dover Flares. A note of sadness, however, was the increasing death toll being inflicted on a war-weary population by the Spanish flu. It killed millions of people across Europe and the British Isles, but the names of its victims are now largely unrecorded and forgotten.

Lord Howard had already given Harehills Park to the town as his own personal recognition of the bravery and sacrifices made by Glossop soldiers and sailors during the Great War. At the end of March in 1922, he was delighted to unveil the official war memorial to those who lost their lives. It was placed on Norfolk Square in the town centre, a tall bronze figure of Victory, holding aloft the symbolic laurels of victory and standing on a high solid stone pillar. The ceremony took place on 31 March. It was a cold and miserable day but the threatened sleet, snow and rain held off until after the unveiling. The memorial, surrounded by 'magnificent floral tributes', was draped in a large Union Jack. The mayor, Samuel Bamforth, and Lord Howard stood proudly side-by-side for the unveiling as the National Anthem and the Last Post were played. Then there was singing followed by the Homeland and Reveille. Mr C. Haughton, who had lost three sons in the war, laid a wreath on behalf of

Private Joseph Cooper of Glossopdale, Royal Welsh Fusiliers, c1916.

all ex-servicemen, and there were wreaths from Mrs Partington, who had been the mayoress during the war years, Glossop Grammar School, the police, and various other organisations. Afterwards the mayor and Lord Howard travelled to neighbouring Hadfield, one of the Glossop townships, for the unveiling of the Hadfield war memorial. The memorial was of a similar style to that of Glossop and stood by Hadfield Hall (now the library) on the corner of Railway Street and Station Road. It too was surrounded by many official and personal 'beautiful floral wreaths'. All who attended the ceremonies stood with bowed heads and prayed that such a terrible war would never happen again.

How long is never? It would be less than twenty years before the world was once again engulfed in a world war.

Index